Child's Talk

Jerome Bruner is also the author of
Beyond the Information Given (*edited by Jeremy M. Anglin*)
The Relevance of Education
Toward a Theory of Instruction

Child's Talk

Learning to Use Language

JEROME BRUNER

With the assistance of Rita Watson

W · W · Norton & Company · *New York* · *London*

FIRST EDITION

The text of this book is composed in photocomposition Baskerville, with display type set in Bodoni. Composition and manufacturing by the Maple-Vail Book Manufacturing Group. Book design by Marjorie J. Flock.

FOR

Roman Jakobson,
visitor from the future

Library of Congress in Publication Data
Bruner, Jerome Seymour.
    Child's Talk: Learning to Use Language.
    Includes bibliographical references and index.
    1. Language acquisition.   2. Children—Language.
I. Title.
P118.B72   1983   401'.9   83-2215

ISBN 0-393-01753-2

ISBN 0-393-95345-9 (pbk.)

W. W. Norton & Company Inc., 500 Fifth Avenue, New York, N.Y. 10110
W. W. Norton & Company Ltd., 37 Great Russell Street, London WC1B 3NU

1 2 3 4 5 6 7 8 9 0

CONTENTS

PREFACE

THIS VOLUME was originally intended to be a collection of selected papers, written in the decade after 1972. The original plan was to rework and to rewrite them individually, to create a book of essays. In the process those earlier papers were absorbed into a more general framework, though traces of them can still be found. They became a single book. Its themes are how the young child acquires the *uses* of his native language and how by using language first for limited ends the child comes finally to recognize its more powerful, productive uses. Its emphasis is on pragmatics—on learning "how to do things with words," in Austin's happy phrase, particularly how to achieve joint attention and conduct joint action with another by the use of language.

I did not begin to study language intensively until 1972, when I moved to Oxford. The developmental linguistics of the decade before that had interested me to be sure, but only as a spectator. Dominated by an interest in syntax and its mastery, it was largely formalistic in spirit. It did not tempt me into the water. It seemed to me lacking in functional force. The focus on grammatical structure found in this style of developmental linguistics seemed to keep it from exploring the functions language served in different contexts and how these functions were developed.

But by the 1970s the study of language acquisition had begun to shift toward a more functional emphasis. It was then that my interest shifted from that of a spectator to that of a participant. A word about that shifting scene is in order. What produced it?

The child, it became clear in spite of earlier claims, had to have some knowledge of the "real" world before he could effectively unravel the mysteries of syntax. Indeed, he used his first syntax for delineating matters of some moment to him. That was the message that reached its first full expression in Roger Brown's magisterial work, *A First Language,* published in 1973. That message became even more evident in the work of Lois Bloom, of Patricia Greenfield, of John Dore—all of whom insisted on the need for "rich interpretation" of child language. Rich interpretation implied the use of context and of communicative function in evaluating the child's syntax. A new functionalism was tempering the formalism of the previous decade.

In Oxford I found the atmosphere dominated by speech act theory. I was already aware of this work from John Austin's work and from Joanna Ryan's early paper on its relevance to the psychology of language. Its emphasis was squarely on *use* and *function*—on illocutionary force as well as on locutionary form. Before long my students, younger colleagues at Oxford, and I were caught up in the psychological implications of speech acts. Before much longer I was sharing the supervision of D. Phil. students with Oxford philosophers in the midst of the new development—my colleagues, Peter Strawson, Anthony Kenney, and Rom Harré. I found them as interested in the psychological issues as I was in the philosophical ones.

In 1974 my friend Niko Tinbergen won the Zwammerdam Medal, and one of the perquisites of that honor was to organize a seminar in Amsterdam as part of the award ceremony. He very kindly invited me to present a paper at "his" Zwammerdam seminar. Tinbergen was passionately interested in the biology of communication—but wary of "grammarian linguistics" as he once called it. I thought this would be a fine occasion to tell him about speech acts. I would use the opportunity to pass on to him my churning thoughts about speech acts and their development, the outcome of a year of preliminary observation of children in the first eighteen months of life and of a great deal of reading and discussion. That was the start of this volume—a paper on the "ontogenesis of speech acts," which duly appeared in 1974.

The observational work continued and so did the discussion. It soon became necessary to bring some clearer order into the maze of issues raised in the Zwammerdam paper. Some people write in order to find out what they think, I among them. And so a second paper—a next step en route to this volume, "From Communication to Language," which appeared in *Cognition* in celebration of Roman Jakobson's eightieth birthday. That paper in turn underwent revision, and the result was another presented in Paris in the summer of 1975: "A Preface to the Development of Speech." It was the game plan for the empirical work that was to follow. By then I had decided that you could only study language acquisition at home, *in vivo*, not in the lab, *in vitro*. The issues of context sensitivity and the format of the mother-child interaction had already led me to desert the handsomely equipped but contrived video laboratory in South Parks Road in favor of the clutter of life at home. We went to the children rather than having them come to us. Intellectual work has a natural history a bit like that of anything that grows. And with each succeeding paper, my own views changed and grew.

And so it went. A book is a product not only of an author (and of his students) but of times and places. It was not only Oxford and the 1970s. It was also a world in which many intellectual streams were converging—the philosophical and linguistic ones already mentioned, but also work in psychology and anthropology concerned with the contextualization of thought and speech and cultural rules. It was a rich decade for anybody working the pastures of pragmatics. The final form of this volume reflects the period and its places as well as the research on which it is based.

The book begins with two chapters on the theoretical issues that motivated the work. These are followed by three empirical ones that deal respectively with "language games" and with the growth of reference and of request. Reference and request are the two major uses of language on which the empirical research focuses. But the chapter on the role of play and games in the acquisition of language is propaedeutic to an understanding of

these uses. "Language games," in the classic Wittgensteinian
sense, is not just a metaphor.

The chapter on "games" owes much to the assistance of Virginia Sherwood, Eileen Caudill, and Nancy Ratner. The chapter
on reference draws heavily on work undertaken jointly with Anat
Ninio when, in 1977–78, she was a visiting fellow from the
Hebrew University of Jerusalem working in Oxford. Nancy Ratner and Eileen Caudill also provided much help in this work.
The chapter on the ontogenesis of request was carried out in
collaboration with Carolyn Roy and Nancy Ratner.

The concluding chapter of this volume is, again, a tale of
successive transformations. It went through a long gestation
period. An embryonic version of it was delivered as the Witkin
Lectures at Princeton in 1980. Extensions and revisions were
presented in the autumn of 1981 at the Sixth Boston Child Language Conference and then at the Delaware Conference. In the
spring of 1982 further variants were launched at Brown and at
Pennsylvania.

This volume has led a well traveled life in progress, and I
am grateful to the many people who gave us hospitality during
those years—in both Cambridges, in Moscow, Budapest, New
York, Nijmegen, Toronto, Bristol, Louvain.

There are two threads that stitch together the ideas and data
that make up this book. The first is "external": how the linguistic
community arranges speech encounters so that the young aspirant speaker can get a hold on how to make his own communicative intentions clear and how to penetrate the intentions of
others. The principal vehicle of this assistance is the *format,* the
patterned situations that enable adult and child to cooperate in
the "passing on" of a language. The second thread is more
"internal" and procedural. It is about how communicative intent
is successively transformed through negotiation into increasingly powerful linguistic procedures. The two threads are rather
like the warp and the weft of the book's argument.

I have not attempted to "cover" the vast literature with which
this book connects. It is intended neither as a review nor as a

critique. My aim, rather, was to use the Oxford research in developing a point of view about how young children are assisted in mastering the language they are acquiring. Very early in the enterprise, it was plain that children enjoy a privileged access to language, that the input to them from the linguistic community is systematically arranged. It was equally plain that children, in attempting to use language to achieve their ends, were doing far more than simply mastering a code. They were negotiating procedures and meanings and, in learning to do so, were learning the ways of the culture as well as the ways of its language. I have concentrated my attention on those authors who were concerned with such matters rather than with the literature of language acquisition in general. Indeed, some of the authors who have most engaged my attention are hardly represented in the bibliography at all, principally because they were not actively concerned with child language as such, or even with language. Clifford Geertz and Dan Sperber are good examples: both are concerned with the manner in which culture is acquired through negotiation rather than through the cracking of a code. I found their work enormously suggestive, though neither is mentioned in the text of the book. My seeming neglect of the literature comes not from disrespect but from concentration on a specific goal.

I take delight in expressing warm thanks to the friendly and obstreperous circle of students and colleagues who provided so much stimulation and pleasure during my years at Oxford. John Churcher, Cathy Urwin, Roy Pea, Alison Garton, Paul Bamborough, Christopher Pratt, Arde Denkel, Alan and Ian Leslie, Andy Meltzoff, Susan Sugarman, Alison Gopnik, and José Linaza all engaged in the fray. Anat Ninio, Magda Kalmar, Aidan Macfarlane, and Michael Scaife were postdoctoral fellows. Visiting fellows added immeasurably: David Olson from Toronto, Robert Grieve from St. Andrews, Katherine Nelson from Yale, Claudia de Lemos from Campinas, and Virginia Volterra from Rome. Kathleen Danaher Sylva started the work with me on problems of reference, but our collaboration was diverted to other matters having to do with child development and care. Renira Huxley joined us, but her brief participation in the work was unhappily terminated by her sad and untimely death. The "Friday lunch seminar" was a steady source of sustenance, and the list of participants is too long to cite. But I particularly want to thank Bärbel Inhelder, Richard Cromer, Adrian Fourcin, Natalie Waterson, Gareth Evans, Maureen Shields, and Charles Taylor for their contributions—and Alison Gopnik for her flair in arranging the proceedings.

Among my Oxford colleagues, I particularly want to express my thanks to Isaiah Berlin, Niko Tinbergen, Rom Harré, Jonathan Cohen, Anthony Kenney, Donald Broadbent, Peter Bryant, Harry Judge, and Roy Harris. They were of great help.

Many hours of patient and intelligent labor must go into the transcribing of protocols. Meg Penning-Rowsell was of particular help in this, as was my secretary, Megan Kenyon.

Old friends and colleagues gave aid and advice: George Miller and Roger Brown, Pim Levelt and Eric Wanner, Margaret Donaldson and Henri Tajfel, Annette Karmiloff-Smith and Elena Lieven, among others. During a sabbatical year at the Netherlands Institute for Advanced Study in Holland, I particularly benefited from discussions with David Olson, Melissa Bowerman, Claudia de Lemos, Manny Schegloff, Patricia Greenfield, and our colleagues at the Max-Planck Institute for Psycholinguistics.

Rita Watson helped with the preliminary selection and editing. I am indebted to her not only for the detailed work that goes into such an enterprise, but also for her good judgment and unfailing good humor. The final editing of this volume was undertaken in collaboration with my colleague Carol Fleisher Feldman, with whom I had the privilege of several years of correspondence while the work was in progress. Her contribution has been of immeasurable help to me.

Publishers of the "old school" still exist to the huge benefit of authors and readers. Donald Lamm is one such, and praise be as well to the new generation of the old breed, particularly to Donald Fusting.

And finally, this volume is dedicated to Roman Jakobson. Alas, he died during the final stages of its writing. He was the deepest linguist of his generation and a man of profound generosity as a teacher and friend. I have kept the form of the original dedication rather than changing it "to the memory of . . ." The distinguished Soviet linguist Ivanov said of Jakobson that he was a "visitor from the future," and I have borrowed his phrase to add to my dedication.

JEROME BRUNER

New York
February 1983

ONE

Introduction

Simply having the evidence presented to you is not enough for learning [language]. . . . We must discover what is necessary to get the system to function.

—*Noam Chomsky*

WHEN ONE SAYS THAT a child is acquiring "language," there are at least three senses in which that assertion can be understood. The first is in terms of well-formedness: that he or she is becoming able to make utterances that conform to the rules of grammar. It is a topic that is fraught with perplexity. How does the infant learn? To begin with, the infant's rules of grammar are often not the same as those used by adults around him. Imitation is a lame explanation. And even when he or she speaks in adultlike grammar, it is highly doubtful whether the child has been exposed to enough exemplars of the rules to have learned them by induction. There is something implausible about most views about the acquisition of grammar: whether they be the views of empiricists who think grammar is learned like anything else, or the views of those who claim that there is some sort of innate disposition that fates human beings to be language acquirers. Besides, it seems highly unlikely in the light of our present knowledge that infants learn grammar for its own sake. Its mastery seems always to be instrumental to doing something with words in the real world, if only *meaning* something.

That is the second aspect of language: its capacity to refer and to mean. While it is the case that one can construct utterances that are syntactically well formed but that do not "mean" anything, it is rare that we do so either as children or as mature speakers. How does the child learn to refer and to mean? And to do so, moreover, by the use of lexico-grammatical speech? It is by no means obvious. For it is obscure what any utterance refers to and means independently of the contexts and conditions in which it is uttered. Even (or especially) single-word utterances are difficult to interpret: Is the expression *fire* a warning, a referential expression for something seen, or a request for a flame?

So when we say that a child is acquiring language, we must account for another aspect of what is being acquired—that is, its function or communicative intent or how to "get things done with words." Here, the criterion for judging progress in acquisition is not so much well-formedness or sense and reference, but something more like effectiveness. Can the child request, can he indicate, can he ingratiate or promise or support or show respect by the use of communicative means? And can he meet the conditions that the culture places on speakers who would do these things—conditions of preparation, sincerity, essentiality, and affiliation?

These three facets of language that the child must master in order to become a "native speaker"—the language's syntax, semantics, and pragmatics—are obviously not and logically could not be learned independently of each other. Syntax is, perhaps, the most mysterious for (without elaborating on the matter) it constitutes a highly intricate and interdependent set of rules in every language. Even so, the other aspects are no less stunning in their complexity. The three aspects of language, moreover, seem to be learned interdependently as one actually observes the process in real life.

This book is about that interdependence. It takes the view that the three facets are inseparable in the process of acquisition—that they are *necessarily* inseparable. More specifically, language acquisition "begins" before the child utters his first lexicogrammatical speech. It begins when mother and infant create a predictable format of interaction that can serve as a microcosm for communicating and for constituting a shared reality. The transactions that occur in such formats constitute the "input" from which the child then masters grammar, how to refer and mean, and how to realize his intentions communicatively.

But he could not achieve these prodigies of language acquisition without, at the same time, possessing a unique and predisposing set of language-learning capacities—something akin to what Noam Chomsky has called a Language Acquisition Device, LAD. But the infant's Language Acquisition Device could not function without the aid given by an adult who enters with him into a transactional format. That format, initially under the control of the adult, provides a Language Acquisition Support System, LASS. It frames or structures the input of language and interaction to the child's Language Acquisition Device in a manner to "make the system function." In a word, it is the interaction between LAD and LASS that makes it possible for the infant to enter the linguistic community—and, at the same time, the culture to which the language gives access.

The remainder of this book is an amplification of how this process works with respect to a pair of communicative functions—referring and requesting—in a pair of young English-speaking children in their first two years of life. I have chosen to examine the transition period from prelinguistic communication to early lexico-grammatical speech, for it best reveals, I believe, some of the crucial processes and key events required for the mastery of language in its three aspects.

From Communicating
to Talking

I F WE ARE TO CONSIDER the transition from prelinguistic communication to language, particularly with a concern for possible continuities, we had better begin by taking as close a look as we can at the so-called "original endowment" of human beings. Might that endowment affect the acquisition and early use of language? I do not mean simply the prelinguistic precursors of grammar or an "innate capacity" for language. The question must be a more general one. What predisposes a living being to use language and be changed by its use? Suppose we grant that there is some innate capacity to master language as a symbolic system, as Noam Chomsky urged, or even to be predisposed toward particular linguistic distinctions, as Derek Bickerton has recently proposed? Why is language used? After all, chimpanzees have some of the same capacities and they don't use them.

The awkward dilemma that plagues questions about the original nature and later growth of human faculties inheres in the unique nature of human competence. For human competence is both biological in origin and cultural in the means by which it finds expression. While the *capacity* for intelligent action has deep biological roots and a discernible evolutionary history, the *exercise* of that capacity depends upon man appropriating to himself modes of acting and thinking that exist not in his genes but in his culture. There is obviously something in "mind" or in "human nature" that mediates between the genes and the culture that makes it possible for the latter to be a prosthetic device for the realization of the former.

When we ask then about the endowment of human beings, the question we put must be twofold. We must ask not only about capacities, but also about how humans are aided in expressing them in the medium of culture. The two questions, of course, are inseparable, since human intellectual capacity necessarily evolved to fit man for using the very prosthetic devices that a culture develops and accumulates for the enablement of its members.

There is some point in studying early human capacities and their development in seemingly cultureless laboratories, as if they were simply expressions of man's biological dispositions and endowment. But we must also bear in mind that the realization of this endowment depends on the tool kit of the culture, whatever we choose to do in the laboratory. The main trend of the last quarter century has been to look increasingly at the contexts that enable human beings to act as they do; increasingly, we can see the futility of considering human nature as a set of autonomous dispositions.

I can easily outline what seems to me, at least, to be "infant endowment" in the so-called cognitive sphere. But to do so relevantly I must focus on those aspects that fit and perhaps even compel human beings to operate in the culture. For I think that it is the requirement of *using* culture as a necessary form of coping that forces man to master language. Language is the means for interpreting and regulating the culture. The interpreting and negotiating start the moment the infant enters the human scene. It is at this stage of interpretation and negotiation that language acquisition is acted out. So I shall look at "endowment" from the point of view of how it equips the infant to come on stage in order to acquire the means for taking his place in culture.

Initial Cognitive Endowment

Let me begin with some more or less "firm" conclusions about perception, skill, and problem solving in the prelinguistic infant and consider how they might conceivably predispose the child to acquire "culture" through language.

The first of these conclusions is that much of the cognitive processing going on in infancy appears to operate in support of goal-directed activity. From the start, the human infant is *active* in seeking out regularities in the world about him. The child is active in a uniquely human way, converting experience into species-typical means-end structures. Let me begin with the unlikely example of non-nutritive sucking.

The human infant, like mammals generally, is equipped with a variety of biological processes that ensure initial feeding, initial attachment to a caretaker, initial sensory contact with the world—all quite well buffered to prevent the infant from overreacting. Nonnutritive sucking, an example of one of these buffering mechanisms, has the effect of relaxing large muscle groups, stilling movements of the gut, reducing the number of eye movements in response to excessively patterned visual fields, and in general assuring the maintenance of a moderate level of arousal in the face of even a demanding environment. That much is probably "hard-wired."

But such sucking soon comes under the child's own control. Infants as young as five to six weeks are quite capable, we found, of sucking on a pacifier nipple in order to bring a visual display from blur into focus—increasing their rate of sucking well above baseline when the picture's focus is made contingent on speed of sucking. Sucking and looking, moreover, are coordinated to assure a good view. When babies suck to produce clarity, they suck as they look, and when they stop they soon learn to look away. The same infants, when their sucking in a later session produces blur, suck while looking away from the blurred picture their sucking is producing and desist from sucking while looking at the picture. (We should note, by the way, that infants do not like blurred pictures.)

The Czech pediatrician Hanus Papousek has reported the same capacity for coordination of action in another domain, head turning. He taught six-to-ten-week-old babies to turn their heads to the right (or the left) in order to activate an attractive set of flashing lights. The infants soon learned the required response and, indeed, could even be taught to turn twice to each side for the desired lights. With mastery, their reactions became quite economical: They turned just enough to bring on the lights. But

more interesting still, as the experiment progressed and the light
display became familiar, they looked at it only briefly, just enough
of a glance to confirm that the lights had gone on as expected
(following which there was often a smile) and would then begin
visually exploring other features of the situation. Successful prediction seems finally to have been the rewarding feature of the
situation. With habituation, performance deteriorated—prediction was no longer interesting.

The point is not that infants are cleverer than was suspected
before. Rather, it is that their behavior from early on is guided
by active means-end readiness and by search. To put it another
way, more in keeping with our general point, the infant from
the start is tuned to the coordinative requirements of action. He
seems able to appreciate, so to speak, the structure of action and
particularly the manner in which means and ends must be combined in achieving satisfactory outcomes—even such arbitrary
means as sucking to produce changes in the visual world. He
seems, moreover, to be sensitive to the requirements of prediction and, if Papousek's interpretation of the "smile of predictive
pleasure" is to be taken seriously, to get active pleasure from
successful prediction. Anyone who has bothered to ponder the
pleasure infants derive from achieving repetitive, surefire prediction will appreciate this point.

To say that infants are also "social" is to be banal. They are
geared to respond to the human voice, to the human face, to
human action and gesture. Their means-end readiness is easily
and quickly brought into coordination with the actions of their
caretakers. The pioneering work of Daniel Stern and Berry Brazelton and their colleagues underlines how early and readily
activated infants are by the adults with whom they interact and
how quickly their means-end structuring encompasses the actions
of another. The infant's principal "tool" for achieving his ends
is another familiar human being. In this respect, human infants
seem more socially interactive than any of the Great Apes, perhaps to the same degree that Great Apes are more socially interactive than Old or New World Monkeys, and this may be a

function of their prolonged and uniquely dependent form of immaturity, as I have argued elsewhere.

Infants are, in a word, tuned to enter the world of human action. Obvious though the point may seem, we shall see that it has enormous consequences for the matter at hand. This leads directly to the second conclusion about infant "endowment."

It is obvious that an enormous amount of the activity of the child during the first year and a half of life is extraordinarily social and communicative. Social interaction appears to be both self-propelled and self-rewarding. Many students of infant behavior, like Tom Bower, have found that a social response to the infant is the most powerful reinforcer one can use in ordinary learning experiments. And withholding social response to the child's initiatives is one of the most disruptive things one can do to an infant—e.g., an unresponding face will soon produce tears. Even in the opening weeks of life the infant has the capacity to imitate facial and manual gestures (as Andrew Meltzoff has shown); they respond with distress if their mothers are masked during feeding; and, they show a sensitivity to expression in the mother by turn taking in vocalization when their level of arousal is moderate and by simultaneous expression when it is high.

While the child's attachment to the mother (or caretaker) is initially assured by a variety of innate response patterns, there very quickly develops a reciprocity that the infant comes to anticipate and count on. For example, if during play the mother assumes a sober immobile face, the infant shows fewer smiles and turns his head away from the mother more frequently than when the mother responds socially, as Edward Tronick and his colleagues have shown. The existence of such reciprocity—buttressed by the mother's increasing capacity to differentiate an infant's "reasons" for crying as well as by the infant's capacity to anticipate these consistencies—soon creates a form of mutual attention, a harmony or "intersubjectivity," whose importance we shall take up later.

In any case, a pattern of inborn initial social responses in the infant, elicited by a wide variety of effective signs from the mother—her heartbeat, the visual configuration of her face and particularly her eyes, her characteristic smell, the sound and rhythms of her voice—is soon converted into a very complex joint anticipatory system that converts initial biological attachment between mother and child into something more subtle and more sensitive to individual idiosyncracies and to forms of cultural practice.

The third conclusion is that much of early infant action takes place in constrained, familiar situations and shows a surprisingly high degree of order and "systematicity." Children spend most of their time doing a very limited number of things. Long periods are spent in reaching and taking, banging and looking, etc. Within any one of these restricted domains, there is striking "systematicity." Object play provides an example. A single act (like banging) is applied successively to a wide range of objects. Everything on which the child can get his hands is banged. Or the child tries out on a single object all the motor routines of which he or she is capable—grasping the object, banging it, throwing it to the floor, putting it in the mouth, putting it on top of the head, running it through the entire repertory.

Nobody has done better than Jean Piaget in characterizing this systematicity. The older view that pictured the infant as "random" in his actions and saw growth as consisting of becoming "coordinated" can no longer stand up to the evidence. Given the limits of the child's range of action, what occurs within that range is just as orderly and systematic as is adult behavior. There may be differences of opinion concerning the "rules" that govern this orderly behavior, but there can be no quarrel about its systematicity. Whether one adopts a Piagetian view of the matter or one more tuned to other theories, like Heinz Werner's, is, in light of the more general issues, quite irrelevant.

It is not the least surprising, in light of this conclusion, that infants enter the world of language and of culture with a readiness to find or invent systematic ways of dealing with social requirements and linguistic forms. The child reacts "culturally" with characteristic hypotheses about what is required and enters language with a readiness for order. We shall, of course, have much more to say about this later.

There are two important implications that follow from this. The first is obvious, though I do not recall ever having encountered the point. It is that from the start, the child becomes readily attuned to "making a lot out of a little" by combination. He typically works on varying a small set of elements to create a larger range of possibilities. Observations of early play behavior and of the infant's communicative efforts certainly confirm this "push" to generativeness, to combinatorial and variational efforts. Indeed, Ruth Weir's classic study of the child's spontaneous speech while alone in his crib after bedtime speaks volumes on this combinatorial readiness, as does Melissa Bowerman's on children's spontaneous speech errors.

The second implication is more social. The acquisition of prelinguistic and linguistic communication takes place, in the main, in the highly constrained settings to which we are referring. The child and his caretaker readily combine elements in these situations to extract meanings, assign interpretations, and infer intentions. A decade ago there was considerable debate among developmental linguists on whether in writing "grammars" of child speech one should use a method of "rich interpretation"—taking into account not only the child's actual speech but also the ongoing actions and other elements of the context in which speech was occurring. Today we take it for granted that one must do so. For it is precisely the combining of all elements in constrained situations (speech and nonspeech alike) that provides the road to communicative effectiveness. It is for this reason that I shall place such heavy emphasis on the role of "formats" in the child's entry into language.

A fourth conclusion about the nature of infant cognitive endowment is that its systematic character is surprisingly abstract. Infants during their first year appear to have rules for dealing with space, time, and even causation. A moving object that is transformed in appearance while it is moving behind a screen produces surprise when it reappears in a new guise. Objects that seem to be propelled in ways that *we* see as unnatural (e.g., without being touched by an approaching object) also produce surprise reactions in a three-month-old as well. Objects explored by touch alone are later recognized by vision alone. The infant's perceptual world, far from being a blooming, buzzing confusion, is rather orderly and organized by what seem like highly abstract rules.

Again, it was Piaget who most compellingly brought this "abstractness" to our attention in describing the logical structure of the child's search for invariance in his world—the search for what remains unchanged under the changing surface of appearance. And again, it is not important whether the "logic" that he attributed to this systematic action is correct or not. What is plain is that, whether Piagetian logical rules characterize early "operational behavior" or whether it can be better described by some more general logical system, we know that cognitively and communicatively there is from the start a capacity to "follow" abstract rules.

It is *not* the case that language, when it is encountered and then used, is the first instance of abstract rule following. It is not, for example, in language alone that the child makes such distinctions as those between specific and nonspecific, between states and processes, between "punctual" acts and recurrent ones, between causative and noncausative actions. These abstract distinctions, picked up with amazing speed in language acquisition, have analogues in the child's way of ordering his world of experience. Language will serve to specify, amplify, and expand distinctions that the child has already about the world. But these abstract distinctions are already present, even without language.

These four cognitive "endowments"—means-end readiness, transactionality, systematicity, and abstractness—provide foundation processes that aid the child's language acquisition. None of them "generates" language, for language involves a set of phonological, syntactic, semantic, and illocutionary rules and maxims that constitute a problem space of their own. But linguistic or communicative hypotheses depend upon these capacities as enabling conditions. Language does not "grow out of" prior protophonological, protosyntactic, protosemantic, or protopragmatic knowledge. It requires a unique sensitivity to a patterned sound system, to grammatical constraints, to referential requirements, to communicative intentions, etc. Such sensitivity grows in the process of fulfilling certain general, nonlinguistic functions—predicting the environment, interacting transactionally, getting to goals with the aid of another, and the like. These functions are first fulfilled primitively if abstractly by prelinguistic communicative means. Such primitive procedures, I will argue, must reach requisite levels of functioning before *any* Language Acquisition Device (whether innate or acquired) can begin to generate "linguistic hypotheses."

Entry into Language

We can turn now to the development of language per se. Learning a native language is an accomplishment within the grasp of any toddler, yet discovering how children do it has eluded generations of philosophers and linguists. Saint Augustine believed it was simple. Allegedly recollecting his own childhood, he said, "When they named any thing, and as they spoke turned towards it, I saw and remembered that they called what one would point out by the name they uttered. . . . And thus by constantly hearing words, as they occurred in various sentences, I collected gradually for what they stood; and having broken in my mouth to these signs, I thereby gave utterance to my will." But a look at children as they actually acquire language shows Saint Augustine to be far, far off target. Alas, he had a powerful effect both on his followers and on those who set out to refute him.

Developmental linguistics is now going through rough times that can be traced back to Saint Augustine as well as to the reactions against him. Let me recount a little history. Saint Augustine's view, perhaps because there was so little systematic research on language acquisition to refute it, prevailed for a long time. It was even put into modern dress. Its most recent "new look" was in the form of behaviorist "learning theory." In this view's terms, nothing particularly linguistic needed to be said about language. Language, like any other behavior, could be "explained" as just another set of responses. Its principles and its research paradigms were not derived from the phenomena of language but from "general behavior." Learning tasks, for example, were chosen to construct theories of learning so as to ensure that the learner had no predispositions toward or knowledge of the material to be learned. All was as if *ab initio,* transfer of response from one stimulus to another was assured by the similarity between stimuli. Language learning was assumed to be much like, say, nonsense syllable learning, except that it might be aided by imitation, the learner imitating the performance of the "model" and then being reinforced for correct performance. Its emphasis was on "words" rather than on grammar. Consequently, it missed out almost entirely in dealing with the combinatorial and generative effect of having a syntax that made possible the routine construction of sentences never before heard and that did not exist in adult speech to be imitated. A good example is the Pivot-Open class, P(0), construction of infant speech in which a common word or phrase is combined productively with other words as in *all-gone mummy, all-gone apple,* and even *all-gone bye-bye* (when mother and aunt finally end a prolonged farewell).

It is one of the mysteries of Kuhnian scientific paradigms that this empiricist approach to language acquisition persisted in psychology (if not in philosophy, where it was overturned by Frege and Wittgenstein) from its first enunciation by Saint Augustine to its most recent one in B. F. Skinner's *Verbal Behavior.* It would be fair to say that the persistence of the mindless behavioristic version of Augustinianism finally led to a readiness, even a reckless readiness, to be rid of it. For it was not only an inadequate account, but one that damped inquiry by its domination of "common sense." It set the stage for the Chomskyan revolution.

It was to Noam Chomsky's credit that he boldly proclaimed the old enterprise bankrupt. In its place he offered a challenging, if counterintuitive hypothesis based on nativism. He proposed that the acquisition of the *structure* of language depended upon a Language Acquisition Device (LAD) that had as its base a universal grammar or a "linguistic deep structure" that humans know innately and without learning. LAD was programmed to recognize in the surface structure of any natural language encountered its deep structure or universal grammar by virtue of the kinship between innate universal grammar and the grammar of any and all natural languages. LAD abstracted the grammatical realization rules of the local language and thus enabled the aspirant speaker potentially to generate all the well-formed utterances possible in the language and none that were ill-formed. The universal grammatical categories that programmed LAD were in the innate structure of the mind. No prior nonlinguistic knowledge of the world was necessary, and no privileged communication with another speaker was required. Syntax was independent of knowledge of the world, of semantic meaning, and of communicative function. All the child needed was exposure to language, however fragmentary and uncontextualized his samples of it might be. Or more correctly, the acquisition of syntax could be conceived of as progressing with the assistance of whatever *minimum* world knowledge or privileged communication proved necessary. The only constraints on rate of linguistic development were psychological limitations on *performance:* the child's limited but growing attention and memory span, etc. Linguistic *competence* was there from the start, ready to express itself when performance constraints were extended by the growth of requisite skills.

It was an extreme view. But in a stroke it freed a generation of psycholinguists from the dogma of association-cum-imitation-cum-reinforcement. It turned attention to the problem of rule learning, even if it concentrated only on syntactic rules. By declaring learning theory dead as an explanation of language acquisition (one of the more premature obituaries of our times), it opened the way for a new account.

George Miller put it well. We now had *two* theories of language acquisition: one of them, empiricist associationism, was impossible; the other, nativism, was miraculous. But the void between the impossible and the miraculous was soon to be filled in, albeit untidily and partially.

To begin with, children in fact had and *needed* to have a working knowledge of the world before they acquired language. Such knowledge gave them semantic targets, so to speak, that "corresponded" in some fashion to the distinctions they acquired in their language. A knowledge of the world, appropriately organized in terms of a system of concepts, might give the child hints as to where distinctions could be expected to occur in the language, might even alert him to the distinctions. There were new efforts to develop a generative semantics out of which syntactical hypotheses could presumably be derived by the child. In an extreme form, generative semantics could argue that the concepts in terms of which the world was organized are the same as those that organize language. But even so, the *linguistic* distinctions still had to be mastered. These were not about the *world* but about morphology or syntax or whatever else characterized the linguistic *code*.

The issue of whether rules of *grammar* can somehow be inferred or generalized from the structure of our knowledge of the world is a very dark one. The strong form of the claim insists that syntax can be derived directly from nonlinguistic categories of knowledge in some way. Perhaps the best claim can be made for a case grammar. It is based on the reasonable claim that the concepts of action are innate and primitive. The aspiring language learner already knows the socalled arguments of action: who performed the action, on what object, toward whom, where, by what instrument, and so on. In Charles Fillmore's phrase, "meanings are relativized to scenes," and this involves an "assignment of perspective." Particular phrases impose a perspective on the scene and sentence decisions are perspective decisions. If, for example, the agent of action is perspectively forefronted by some grammatical means such as being inserted as head word, the placement of the nominal that represents agency must be the "deep subject" of the sentence. This leaves many questions unanswered about how the child gets to the point of being able to put together sentences that assign his intended action perspectives to scenes.

The evidence for the semantic account was nonetheless interesting. Roger Brown pointed out, for example, that at the two-word stage of language acquisition more than three-quarters of the child's utterances embody only a half dozen semantic relations that are, at base, case or caselike relations—Agent-Action, Action-Object, Agent-Object, Possession, etc. Do these semantic relations generate the grammar of the language? Case notions of this kind, Fillmore tells us, "comprise a set of universal, presumably innate, concepts which identify certain types of judgments human beings are capable of making about the events that are going on around them . . . who did it, who it happened to, and what got changed." The basic structures are alleged to be these arguments of action, and different languages go about realizing them in different ways: by function words, by inflectional morphemes as in the case endings of Latin, by syntactic devices like passivization, and so on. Grammatical forms might then be the surface structures of language, depending for their acquisition on a prior understanding of deep semantic, indeed even protosemantic, concepts about action.

Patrica Greenfield then attempted to show that the earliest *one-word* utterances, richly interpreted in context, could also be explained as realizations of caselike concepts. And more recently Katherine Nelson has enriched the argument that children acquire language already equipped with concepts related to action: "The functional core model (FCM) essentially proposed that the child came to language with a store of familiar concepts of people and objects that were organized around the child's experience with these things. Because the child's experience was active, the dynamic aspects would be the most potent part of what the child came to know about the things experienced. It could be expected that the child would organize knowledge around what he could do with things and what they could do. In other words, knowledge of the world would be functionally organized from the child's point of view." To this earlier view she has now added a temporal dimension—the child's mastery of "scripts for event structures," a sequential structure of "causally and temporally linked acts with the actors and objects specified in the most general way." These scripts provide the child with a set of syntagmatic formats that permit him to organize his concepts sequentially into sentencelike forms such as those reported by Roger Brown. The capacity to do this rests upon a basic form of representation that the child uses from the start and gradually elaborates. In effect, it is what guides the formation of utterances beyond the one-word stage.

The role of world knowledge in generating or supporting language acquisition is now undergoing intensive study. But still another element has now been added—the pragmatic. It is the newest incursion into the gap between "impossible" and "miraculous" theories of language acquisition. In this view, the central idea is communicative intent: we communicate with some end in mind, some function to be fulfilled. We request or indicate or promise or threaten. Such functionalism had earlier been a strong thread in linguistics, but had been elbowed aside by a prevailing structuralism that, after Ferdinand de Saussure's monumental work, became the dominant mode.

New developments revived functionalism. The first was in the philosophy of language spearheaded by Ludwig Wittgenstein's use-based theory of meaning, formulated in his *Philosophical Investigations,* and then by the introduction of speech acts in Austin's *How to Do Things with Words.* Austin's argument (as already noted) was that an utterance cannot be analyzed out of the context of its use and its use must include the intention of the speaker and interpretation of that intention by the addressee in the light of communication conventions. A speaker may make a request by many alternative linguistic means, so long as he honors the conventions of his linguistic community. It may take on interrogative construction ("What time is it?"), or it may take the declarative form ("I wonder what time it is").

Roger Brown notes an interesting case with respect to this issue: in the protocols of Adam, he found that Adam's mother used the interrogative in two quite different ways, one as a request for action, the other as a request for information: "Why don't you . . . (e.g., play with your ball now)?" and "Why are you playing with your ball?" Although Adam answered informational *why* questions with *Because,* there was no instance of his ever confusing an action and an information-seeking *why* question. He evidently recognized the differing intent of the two forms of utterance quite adequately from the start. He must have been learning speech acts rather than simply the *why* interrogative form.

This raises several questions about acquisition. It puts pragmatics into the middle of things. Is intent being decoded by the child? It would seem so. But linguistics usually defines its domain as "going from sound to sense." But what is "sense?" Do we in fact go from sound to intention, as John Searle proposed? A second question has to do with shared or conventional presuppositions. If children are acquiring notions about how to interpret the intentions encoded in utterances, they must be taking into account not only the structure of the utterance, but also the nature of the conditions that prevail just at the time the utterance is made. Speech acts have at least three kinds of conditions affecting their appropriateness or "felicity": a preparatory condition (laying appropriate ground for the utterance); an essential condition (meeting the logical conditions for performing a speech act, like, for example, being uninformed as a condition for asking for information related to a matter); and sincerity conditions (wishing to have the information that one asks for). They must also meet affiliative conditions: honoring the affiliation or relation between speaker and hearer, as in requesting rather than demanding when the interlocutor is not under obligation.

Paradoxically, the learning of speech acts may be easier and less mysterious than the learning either of syntax or semantics. For the child's syntactic errors are rarely followed by corrective feedback, and semantic feedback is often lax. But speech acts, on the contrary, get not only immediate feedback but also correction. Not surprising, then, that prelinguistic communicative acts precede lexico-grammatical speech in their appearance. Not surprising, then, that such primitive "speech act" patterns may serve as a kind of matrix in which lexico-grammatical achievements can be substituted for earlier gestural or vocal procedures.

In this view, entry into language is an entry into discourse that requires both members of a dialogue pair to interpret a communication and its intent. Learning a language, then, consists of learning not only the *grammar* of a particular language but also learning how to realize one's intentions by the appropriate use of that grammar.

The pragmatician's stress on intent requires a far more active role on the part of the adult in aiding the child's language acquisition than that of just being a "model." It requires that the adult be a consenting partner, willing to negotiate with the child. The negotiation has to do, probably, least with syntax, somewhat more with the semantic scope of the child's lexicon, and a very great deal with helping make intentions clear and making their expression fit the conditions and requirements of the "speech community," i.e., the culture.

And the research of the last several years—much of it summarized in Catherine Snow and Charles Ferguson's *Talking to Children*—does indeed indicate that parents play a far more active role in language acquisition than simply modeling the language and providing, so to speak, input for a Language Acquisition Device. The current phrase for it is "fine tuning." Parents speak at the level where their children can comprehend them and move ahead with remarkable sensitivity to their child's progress. The dilemma, as Roger Brown puts it, is how do you teach children to talk by talking baby talk with them at a level that they already understand? And the answer has got to be that the important thing is to keep communicating with them, for by so doing one allows them to learn how to extend the speech that they have into new contexts, how to meet the conditions on speech acts, how to maintain topics across turns, how to know what's worth talking about—how indeed to regulate language use.

So we can now recognize two ways of filling the gap between an impossible empiricist position and a miraculous nativist one. The child must master the conceptual structure of the world that language will map—the social world as well as the physical. He must also master the conventions for making his intentions clear by language.

Support for Language Acquisition

The development of language, then, involves two people negotiating. Language is not encountered willy-nilly by the child; it is shaped to make communicative interaction effective—fine-tuned. If there is a Language Acquisition Device, the input to it is not a shower of spoken language but a highly interactive affair shaped, as we have already noted, by some sort of an adult Language Acquisition Support System.

After all, it is well known from a generation of research on another "innate" system, sexual behavior, that much experiential priming is necessary before innate sexual responses can be evoked by "appropriate" environmental events. Isolated animals are seriously retarded. By the same token, the recognition and the production of grammatical universals may similarly depend upon prior social and conceptual experience. Continuities between prelinguistic communication and later speech of the kind I alluded to earlier may, moreover, need an "arranged" input of adult speech if the child is to use his growing grasp of conceptual distinctions and communicative functions as guides to language use. I propose that this "arranging" of early speech interaction requires routinized and familiar settings, formats, for the child to comprehend what is going on, given his limited capacity for processing information. These routines constitute what I intend by a Language Acquisition Support System.

There are at least four ways in which such a Language Acquisition Support System helps assure continuity from prelinguistic to linguistic communication. Because there is such concentration on familiar and routine transactional formats, it becomes feasible for the adult partner to highlight those features of the world that are already salient to the child and that have a basic or simple grammatical form. Slobin has suggested, for example, that there are certain prototypical ways in which the child experiences the world: e.g., a "prototypical transitive event" in which "an animate agent is seen willfully . . . to bring about a physical and perceptible change of state or location in a patient by means of direct body contact." Events of this kind, we shall see, are a very frequent feature of mother-child formats, and it is of no small interest that in a variety of languages, as Slobin notes, they "are encoded in consistent grammatical form by age two." Slobin offers the interesting hypothesis "that [these] prototypical situations are encoded in the most basic grammatical forms available in a language." We shall encounter formats built around games and tasks involving both these prototypical means-end structures and canonical linguistic forms that seem almost designed to aid the child in spotting the referential correspondence between such utterances and such events.

Or to take another example, Bickerton has proposed that children are "bioprogrammed" to notice certain distinctions in real world events and to pick up (or even to invent) corresponding linguistic destinctions in order to communicate about them. His candidates are the distinctions (a) between specific and nonspecific events, (b) between state and process, (c) between "punctual" and continuous events, and (d) between causative and noncausative actions. And insofar as the "fine tuning" of adult interaction with a child concentrates on these distinctions—both in reality and in speech—the child is aided in moving from their conceptual expression to an appreciation of their appropriate linguistic representation. Again, they will be found to be frequent in the formats of the children we shall look at in detail.

A second way in which the adult helps the child through formating is by encouraging and modeling lexical and phrasal substitutes for familiar gestural and vocal means for effecting various communicative functions. This is a feature of the child's gradual mastery of the request mode that we will be exploring in a later chapter.

H. P. Grice takes it as a hallmark of mature language that the speaker not only has an intention to communicate, but that he also has *conventionalized* or "nonnatural" means for expressing his intention. The speaker, in his view, presupposes that his interlocutor will accept his means of communication and will infer his intention from them. The interlocutor presupposes the same thing about the speaker. Grice, concerned with adults, assumes all this to be quite conscious, if implicit.

An infant cannot at the prelinguistic outset be said to be participating in a conscious Gricean cycle when signaling conventionally in his games with his mother. That much self-consciousness seems unlikely. But what we will find in the following chapters is that the mother acts as if he did. The child in turn soon comes to operate with some junior version of the Gricean cycle, awaiting his mother's "uptake" of his signaling.

In Katherine Nelson's terms, the young child soon acquires a small library of scripts and communicative procedures to go with them. They provide steady frameworks in which he learns effectively, by dint of interpretable feedback, how to make his communicative intentions plain. When he becomes "conscious" enough to be said to be operating in a Gricean cycle is, I think, a silly question.

What is striking is how early the child develops means to signal his focus of attention and his requests for assistance—to signal them by conventionalized means in the limited world of familiar formats. He has obviously picked up the gist of "nonnatural" or conventionalized signaling of his intentions before ever he has mastered the formal elements of lexico-grammatical speech. I think the reader will agree, in reading later chapters, that the functional framing of communication starts the child on his way to language proper.

Thirdly, it is characteristic of play formats particularly that they are made of stipulative or constitutive "events" that are created by language and then recreated on demand by language. Later these formats take on the character of "pretend" situations. They are a rich source of opportunity for language learning and language use and, again, we shall have a closer look at one such in a later chapter.

Finally, once the mother and child are launched into routinized formats, various psychological and linguistic processes are brought into play that generalize from one format to another. Naming, for example, appears first in indicating formats and then transfers to requesting formats. Indeed, the very notion of finding linguistic parallels for conceptual distinctions generalizes from one format to another. So too do such "abstract" ideas as segmentation, interchangeable roles, substitutive means—both in action and in speech.

These are the mundane procedures and events that constitute a Language Acquisition Support System, along with the elements of fine tuning that comprise "baby talk" exchanges.

That much said, we can turn to the details.

THREE

Play, Games, and Language

SEVERAL YEARS AGO I undertook a study of the evolution of the nature and uses of immaturity in the various primate species. A major conclusion of that survey was that "one concomitant of the [evolutionary] change is the decline of fixed patterns of induction into the group. There is much less of what might be called training by threat from adults or punishment by adults of a juvenile who has violated a species typical pattern. The prolonged infant-mother interaction includes now a much larger element of play between them, often initiated by the mother and often used to divert an infant from a frustration-arousing situation." I commented at that time on the various important functions that play serves among immature members of higher primate species: minimizing the severity of the consequences of action; offering an opportunity for trying out "combinations of behavior that would, under functional pressure, never be tried"; and in general loosening up or "dissociating" fixed relations that might have existed between means and ends in instrumental behavior. A principal conclusion of that study was that the increased dominance of play during immaturity among Great Apes and Hominids served as a preparation for the technical-social life that constitutes human culture.

But nowhere below Man does one find the "games" of childhood and infancy that are the staple and delight of human immaturity—the peekaboo variants, Ride-a-Cock-Horse, This-is-the-Way-the-Ladies-Ride, and the rest. For all of them depend in some measure upon the use and exchange of language. They are games that are constituted by language and can exist only where language is present.

Such games make several other distinctive contributions to human immaturity. They often provide the first occasion for the child's systematic use of language with an adult. They offer the first opportunity to explore how to get things done with words. For the words of play are virtually pure performatives. And as with his primate ancestors, the child can explore without serious consequences for himself, can do so in a limited arena for combinatorial activity that also allows him to dissociate means and ends in the sense that there are various ways of getting to his goals. Like the word games made famous by Ludwig Wittgenstein in his *Philosophical Investigations,* each of the games that are played by children and their parents is a self-contained "form of life" as well. The games are, in a word, an idealized and closely circumscribed format.

I call them "idealized" for several reasons. To begin with, as already noted, they are constitutive and self-contained. Even their goal is constituted by the game itself: the reappearance of a face from behind a screen accompanied by a voiced *boo!* has no functional significance outside the "form of life" that is the game of peekaboo. In this sense, a game is virtually syntactic: its object is to be well formed. It is, moreover, completely conventional and "nonnatural." Even if peekaboo depended for its force upon the child's uncertainty about object permanence (which it may well do), it is nonetheless composed of completely made up, factitious constituents and tied together by a set of only slightly negotiable rules. And, of course, it is made up, precisely, of a set of constituent acts that are formed in sequence in a particular order and transformed with regard to the rules as well. Game formats, moreover, may be conceived of as having a "deep structure" and a set of realization rules by which the surface of the game is managed. The deep structure of peekaboo is the controlled disappearance and reappearance of an object or a person. The surface structure (as we shall see) can be constructed by the use of screens or cloths or whatnot, by varying the time and action between disappearance and reappearance, by varying the constitutive utterance used, by varying who or what is cause to disappear, etc. The idealization, indeed, makes the format almost "languagelike."

Such games also include another design feature of language—the assignment of turn-taking roles that are inter-changeable. There is a hider and a hidden, an actor and an experiencer. And these can be exchanged from game to game. The "meaning" or signaling value of any act or utterance in the game depends, besides, on where in the sequence it occurs and by whom it is done. A game, in its way, is a little protoconversation.

And finally (the point is not a minor one), games provide an opportunity for distributing attention over an ordered sequence of events. The game is the topic about which each of the moves may be considered a comment. And some comments, indeed, are not acceptable to the child: some variants that "push" the game beyond its rule limits will be objected to. Specific elements of the game are being constantly evaluated in terms of their relations to the more extended sequence that "carries" the game, and this too is very languagelike.

And (as if it needed saying!) children love to play, and at the tender age with which we are concerned, they love to play games. There seems to be the same *Funktionslust,* Karl Buhler's word for pleasure in the activity itself, about game playing as there is about early talking. Whatever motivates such process pleasure, it serves the child well in keeping him at it.

At what? At some surprisingly complex activity, as we shall see in a moment.

Two Case Studies: Richard and Jonathan

Richard and Jonathan, whose language development will be the center of our attention throughout the remainder of the book, were studied at home once a fortnight and sometimes more often when things were moving fast or when their parents had noticed something they thought we should be looking at. We began the observations when Richard was five months old and Jonathan three months. Each fortnight we (one of two other observers and I or the two others together) would visit their homes for about an hour and make half-hour video and audio tapes of the mother and child playing at what happened then to be their usual playtime activity. These visits continued until Richard was twenty-four months old and Jonathan eighteen months.

The children were from middle-class homes—their fathers were a schoolmaster and a physician respectively, their mothers housewives who had not attended university. We observers became friendly with the families over the year or so of association, and though we stayed in the background during the recording session, we did respond naturally to the approaches of the children or their parents. The parents kept notebooks and recorded new forms of speech when they emerged, though these were not subjected to detailed analysis. From the start we made it clear that we were studying language development and shared with the parents, when they asked, any ideas or hypotheses we had about their children's development. It was as open a relationship as possible. They were interested in the general course of the study, though not very interested in the technical details.

Video and audio tapes were transcribed as soon after recording as possible, usually within a week, aided by context notes and memory. The transcripts took the usual three-column form of temporally ordered notations of mother's utterances, child's utterances, and context descriptions. These then served as the data base for analysis and categorization of utterances, aided by further viewing of the tapes to resolve ambiguities as they arose. Since much of the technical detail of the particular studies has been published elsewhere, the reader can be spared a tedious recounting of the rather traditional method of analysis employed.

The "games" selected for discussion here were all built around the appearance and disappearance of objects. Jonathan, whom we shall consider first, was very taken with such "games." Whatever the "motivation" of the game—whether a concern with "object permanence," as suggested earlier, or with other aspects of achieving predictability—Jonathan's mother could count on his interest and very early began to elaborate a game composed of predictably linked segments. This game involved a little toy clown that could be moved so as to rise above or disappear into a cloth cone mounted on a stick. It was first played when Jonathan was 0;5—after he and his mother had been playing a "direct" peekaboo game for two months in which the mother, principally, either hid her own face or Jonathan's.*

At the start, Jonathan was little more than a smiling spectator as the clown disappeared and then reappeared. He soon began to anticipate what would happen next. The clown and cone game continued, along with other forms of peekaboo, until 0;9, disappeared, and then reappeared at 1;2 of which more presently.

A single game comprised an Antecedent Topic and a Subsequent Topic, the former consisting of the clown's initial disappearance, and the latter of his reappearance. Each of these Topics was composed of two components. The components of the Antecedent Topic were PREPARATION and DISAPPEARANCE; those of the Subsequent Topic were REAPPEARANCE and REESTABLISHMENT. Each component consisted of two or more constituents by which a component could be "realized" in actual behavior or utterance. The overall structure of the game is presented in Table 3.1, along with examples of each of the ten constituents that make up this "surface structure" to which the child was exposed.

Each constituent was segmented by a pause or some other appropriate means for marking it off from the next constituent. The pauses or other markings between the four components were longer or more salient. And the pause between Antecedent and Subsequent Topics was particularly long and pregnant with suspense. Those are the structural bones of the game. Let me illustrate them less abstractly—in the spirit of the illustrations given at the bottom of the "game tree."

PREPARATION involves an initial constituent in which the mother first calls the child's attention to the clown by jiggling it around or using some such *Attentional vocative* as *Who's this?* with

---

*The expression 0;5 refers to five months; 1;2.10 to one year, two months, and ten days, etc. We follow this convention throughout.

Game

Antecedent topic — Subsequent topic

PREPARATION　**DISAPPEARANCE**　**REAPPEARANCE**　**REESTABLISHMENT**

Attentional vocative　*Agency establishment*　*Start*　*Completion*　*Search*　*Start*　*Completion*　*Start*　*Finish*　*Arousal*　*Constraint*

Jonathan, look what I've got here.
Who's this?

Shall Mummy hide him?
Jonathan do it.

He's going. He's going to go-o-o.

Gone! He's gone!

Where's he gone?

Here he comes.
He's coming to see you.

Boo!
Hello, Jonathan.

There he is.

Babababoo! (moving clown to his belly).

Don't eat him.

a marked interrogative contour. Once attention is gained, the mother settles the question of who is to be agent and who experiencer: *Agency establishment.* Then DISAPPEARANCE begins. It has three constituents. The *Start,* the *Completion,* and the *Search: Here he goes! He's gone! Where is he?* Then there is a long pause, followed by the *Start* of REAPPEARANCE, which can be handled either slowly or explosively, followed then by *Completion: He's coming. Boo, Jonathan! Here he is.* Then, after another pause, the REESTABLISHMENT component begins with *Arousal* when the mother attempts to excite Jonathan with the clown, followed by *Constraint* when she succeeds: *Bababoo* (moving the clown toward him)! *Oh, don't eat him!* All of the constituents can be but are not always accompanied by words.

What is invariant in the game is its deep structure—disappearance and reappearance of an object. It remains so across a wide range of surface realizations. There is no surprise in the *basic* game. Surprise is always achieved by varying the constituents by which it is realized. These constitents then become realized and marked by moderately predictable (but only moderately) variations in utterance and prosody. For example, the various constituents were rarely all accompanied by mother's vocal utterances. Sometimes only one was so marked. And when the games followed one right after the other, the mother usually accompanied different constituents by their appropriate, familiar vocal accompaniment. It was as if she were purposely creating vocal place holders in the sequence of constituents. The same held for her prosodic marking of the utterances she actually used. They were cunningly varied to produce change and suspense. On REAPPEARANCE, for example, the *Start* would over time be very slow, *Here . . . he . . . comes,* and the next time delivered with breakneck speed. So too with the emergence of the clown. Thus while the overall game became routinized, the constituents that made it up were forever being varied: utterances, prosody, pause lengths, whatever.

Jonathan's "entry" into the game was gradual. From 0;5 to 0;9 he paid increasingly more active attention. His mother altered her role accordingly. The ten constituents that she could mark with a vocalization became increasingly elaborated. Take, for example. *Where's he gone?*, the *Search* constituent. She used this standard question forty-three times between Jonathan's fifth and ninth month. At 0;7, she added to this standard phrase *Where is he?*; at 0;8, *Is he in there? Can you see him?*; and at 0;9, *Where's the clown?* (introducing the nominal)—all supplemental forms. It was evident that as these new features became "expectable," Jonathan would wait for his mother to utter them—looking up at her from the clown-and-cone and smiling either in anticipation or after she spoke. Her richer language was becoming a part of the game. Increasingly, he, too, would vocalize during these junctures between the constituents.

The omission of expected utterances was handled in an interesting way by Jonathan's mother. Early on, she vocally accompanied nearly every constituent of the game. At 0;5, for example, she marked as many as nine of them in one round, seven in another. By 0;9, her utterances had dropped to a maximum of four per game. Three constituents in particular were sacrificed to sustain Jonathan's interest: the start phase of the disappearance (*He's going*); the start phase of the reappearance (*Here he comes*); and the completion of the reappearance (*There he is*). What remained were the quick withdrawal (*Gone!*) and explosive reentry (*Boo!*) and a far greater use of constraints (*Don't eat him* or *No, I don't think you'd better put that in your mouth*)— utterances that by their nature were much more closely tied to the child's actions and presumed intentions and far less ritualized in character. The deletions were paced in such a way that they coincided with Jonathan's mastery of the game. When a constituent, in effect, could be presupposed, the mother's vocalization was deleted. It was a striking way of establishing a convention of presupposition.

Jonathan's responsiveness to his mother's vocalizations also revealed an interesting trend. At 0;5, attempting to grab the clown dominated the scene. By 0;6, he accompanied his attempts to reach or grab the clown with undifferentiated vocalizations.

These were distributed throughout the game. But by 0;7, Jonathan began responding to the game's predictable rhythm. He lost interest in grabbing and now reacted at appropriate points by smiling and laughter. During the *Search* phase right after DISAPPEARANCE, for example, his smiling and vocalizations were "shared" with the mother as they established eye contact while she talked the clown back into REAPPEARANCE.

Soon after, Jonathan began taking a more agentlike role, trying clumsily to produce the disappearance and reappearance himself. No longer pleased to be merely surprised by the clown, by 0;8 he was ready to get the clown up out of the cone by himself. When his mother limited his efforts, his attention lagged. In effect, she was forced to let him take the lead in order to hold his interest. When she failed to yield (as observed on thirteen occasions at 0;8), Jonathan abandoned the game on half the occasions. She gave in and let him take possession of the clown whenever he demanded it. To help him manage this, she condensed the surface structure of the game to two essential constituents (*gone!* at DISAPPEARANCE and *boo!* at REAPPEARANCE). But by 0;9, he was permitted to touch and hold the clown during some constituents of nearly every round. By then, he was vocalizing along with his mother on at least one constituent of every game.

The growth of Jonathan's active, motor participation in the game is described in Table 3.2. At the start, it was mostly unre-

Table 3.2 • PERCENTAGE OF GAMES IN WHICH
JONATHAN HELD, TOUCHED, OR MOUTHED THE CLOWN

Age	Percentage of Games	Total Number of Games
0;5	36	11
0;6	43	23
0;7	6	16
0;8	53	17
0;9	75	8

lated to the structure of the game, as already noted. By 0;7, this random manipulation and grabbing stops—only 6 percent of the rounds contain instances of it. But from then to the end of the ninth month, they increase again. Now, however, they are in tune with the structure of the game.

Finally, toward the end of the ninth month, he became bored. The game was not enough to hold him. It began losing its appeal when his interest in manual exploration began to dominate. He became more interested in the clown-and-cone as a toy than as a game. His attention moved to other objects that gave greater scope to his growing sensory-motor powers. But his interest in appearance and disappearance did not altogether wane. Toward the end of his ninth month peekaboo resurfaced. But it had a new twist. The same deep structure was there, but with a new surface form. His mother would hide a toy animal behind her back, then "surprise" Jonathan with its sudden appearance, marked by her *boo!* Now for the first time Jonathan matched his mother's utterances with a standard one of his own (a labial vibrato, or "raspberry").

From this small beginning, an expanded pattern began to elaborate. A month later his mother hid herself behind a chair and Jonathan waited on the other side, watching, vocalizing, and laughing in anticipation of her reappearance. His vocalizations were simply exuberant calls as she disappeared and reappeared. But note that he regularly *looked away* immediately after her reappearance, but virtually always joined gaze with her *before* her next disappearance. In another two months (midway through his twelfth month), Jonathan hid *himself* behind the same chair. He not only initiated the hiding but terminated it on reappearance with a near-standard *ooo!*. During the same episode, when the experimenter joined in and disappeared, Jonathan cried *gone!* He now could initiate the game as agent, with another in the role of experiencer, and was even able to take on a new experiencer—the experimenter!

Two months later, at 1;2, the clown-and-cone game returned to favor. By then Jonathan could participate as agent *or* as experiencer. But now some negotiating was needed to decide who was to be agent. He preferred the more active role but did not monopolize it. He played it rather well; first ejecting the clown from its cone while vocalizing his variant of *boo!* (*ooo!*), then approximating his mother's *all gone* (*a ga*) while stuffing the clown back into its cone. Finally, he imitated his mother's *peekaboo* with *pick* as he yanked the clown out again and again stuffed it back. When his mother served as agent, Jonathan gestured (raising his arm) and vocalized (*ah*) to signal the reappearance of the clown. He had become master of the game, both as agent and as experiencer. Now together, facing and smiling at each other, Jonathan and his mother called out *boo!* in unison, no matter which one of them had control. Roles had become completely interchangeable. The game itself had also provided a structured format to which Jonathan's burgeoning linguistic powers could be applied. He had learned not only where the vocal performatives fit into the sequence, but what they were and how to say them.

In the course of this play, Jonathan had developed not only some performative language for playing the game, but had learned a great deal about the management of interaction. Russian students of language development, like Alexander Luria, have made much of the importance of bringing "impulsive" action under the control of language. And certainly that is the history of Jonathan, moving from the "grabbiness" of the six-month-old to the highly tuned participation of the year-old. But it is more than language that operates as a controlling factor. It is convention, negotiated conventional ways of proceeding in the game, that dominates. Language, principally as a set of sequenced performatives, is one aspect of this conventionalization. It is surely important, but it is part of a broader pattern of "culture acquisition." Yet, for all that, nonperformative language was also migrating into the game, like the aspectual completive *gone,* and others were to follow. So the conventionalized format of the game was also proving fertile ground for the extension of his lexicon.

With Richard, peekaboo was more personal and direct from the start. Its structure was classic—he or his mother would disappear and reappear from behind a screen. Occasionally a toy was the object in the game. Their games varied more than Jonathan's, Richard's mother being more freewheeling about variations on a theme. Or perhaps "person peekaboo" lends itself more to variation.

Between 0;6 and 0;11, we observed seventy-one games on twenty different occasions. As with the clown-and-cone, their game then went underground, not to surface again until 1;2. We then observed it in altered form for another twenty-nine games until 1;3, when it went underground again. At 1;9 it reappeared, but this time in a form that could be played by Richard alone, without a partner.

Consider the early game (0;6–0;11). Roughly, it exhibited the same "deep structure" as clown-and-cone, though its surface structure more readily permitted Richard to take over the role of agent in all constituents since no manual skill was required. In the beginning, however, agency was almost completely monopolized by the mother (Table 3.3); she always initiated hiding during those early games. By the time the game reappeared at 1;2, the pattern was transformed: nine out of ten times, Richard did the hiding. At reappearance in the early game, the mother again initiated, invariably reappearing with a smile and *hello!* Richard "helped" by reaching toward the mother's mask only one time in five. During the resurfaced game after 1;2, he generally unmasked himself. Later in the first phase, if he did the hiding, which he did increasingly, he did *all* his own unmasking. He had moved from the role of experiencer in the first set of games to that of actor in the second set.

His vocalizations also changed in the second set. In peekaboo one can vocalize *before* or *after* the reappearance of the hidden subject, in *anticipation* or upon *completion* of an act. In the early games Richard's vocalizations were equally divided. In the second set, however, there were six completion vocalizations to one anticipatory (Table 3.3). In the earlier games his vocalizations were invariably excited babbles; in the later ones they were lexemelike in length and contour. At first his sounds were principally diffusely directed; by the time he played later games, they

Table 3.3 • THE STRUCTURE AND ANALYSIS OF
RICHARD'S PEEKABOO GAME

Structure

```
                        Game
              /                    \
      Antecedent topic         Subsequent topic
       /          \             /           \
Preparation  Disappearance  Reappearance  Reestablishment
```

Analysis

PERCENTAGE OF GAMES DURING WHICH MOTHER
OR CHILD INITIATED HIDING

	Richard's Age	
	0;6–0;11	1;2–1;3
Mother initiated hiding	100.0	21.9
Child initiated hiding	—	78.1
	(73 games)	(32 games)

PERCENTAGE OF GAMES DURING WHICH THE MOTHER,
THE CHILD, OR AN OBJECT WAS HIDDEN

	Richard's Age	
	0;6–0;11	1;2–1;3
Mother hidden	43.8	6.2
Child hidden	28.8	93.8
Object hidden	27.4	—
	(73 games)	(32 games)

PERCENTAGE OF GAMES DURING WHICH MOTHER, CHILD,
OR BOTH REMOVED MASK

	Richard's Age	
	0;6–0;11	1;2–1;3
Mother removed mask	75.3	12.5 ·
Child removed mask	24.7	78.1
Both removed mask	—	9.4
	(73 games)	(32 games)

PERCENTAGE OF GAMES DURING WHICH CHILD'S VOCALIZATIONS
OCCURRED BEFORE OR AFTER REAPPEARANCE PHASE

	Richard's Age	
	0;6–0;11	1;2–1;3
Before reappearance	20.5	6.2
After reappearance	20.5	37.5
No vocalizations	63.0	56.2
	(73 games)	(32 games)

were directed to his partner. They included such "words" as (at 1;3.21), *peeboo, da, hi da, dere, ahh.* Since many of these were also used in contexts other than peekaboo, functioning as greetings (*hi*) or demonstratives (*ahh, da, dere*), it is possible that by the later games, peekaboo was no longer a self-contained format. The migration of *hi* and *da* into peekaboo suggests that the game was being opened to make way for general greeting and demonstratives.

Indeed, during the three-month demise of peekaboo (0;11–1;2), Richard had begun another appearance-disappearance format involving active search for objects hidden inside containers or closed fists. The hiding was always done by an adult—his mother or the experimenter—and the searching and finding by Richard himself. Perhaps it *was* a form of peekaboo, but I doubt it, for its "drama" was very different. It seemed more a "guessing game."

When peekaboo proper reappeared yet again at 1;2, Richard took total control of the role of agent. On first occurrence, he watched his mother hide her face behind a videotape box twice and then "took over." He hid his own face behind the same box sixteen times consecutively, each time responding to his partner's *boo!* on his reappearance with a smile and an occasional vocalization. By 1;3, the game had been converted into an even more active form; Richard no longer hid behind a box or put a cloth in front of his face, but actually moved behind a sofa or chair to "disappear," then reappearing the same way. He had easily incorporated walking into the slots of the game that before required only moving a screen before his face. In fact, the new game also incorporated elements of hide-and-seek as well, for he also varied where he hid.

After 1;3, Richard and his mother rarely played peekaboo in any usual sense of the game. But object hiding continued. Yet peekaboo surfaced six months later (1;9.14), after Richard had acquired a fair amount of language. This time, however, it was a solo game, between Richard and objects *he* had hidden and then caused to reappear. In spite of this change, the game was still standardly ritualized, even though it was a "pretend" game in which reappearing objects were greeted socially as if they were people. Richard, for example, filled a large kettle with pieces from a puzzle. He then greeted each piece with *hello house!* when he spied it in the pot that he uncovered, sharing a smile or laugh with his mother as he did so. He repeated the routine again and again, each *hello house* followed by a *bye-bye house* as he replaced the lid. Once during this routine, the doorbell rang. Richard swung around, pointed to the door, calling out *hello!*, experiencing no difficulty in shifting from the pretend "hellos" of the game to the conventional mode of greeting. He could use his contrastive *hello* and *bye-bye* systematically either in a game or in real greeting and departure. He could also handle the interchangeable roles involved with ease. The following month, for example, he called out *Where mummy?* when she hid and then *hello* when she reappeared—much as she would have done had she controlled the game.

The final episode in the saga of Richard's peekaboo occurred at 1;11.14. He had lost an object behind the sofa cushion. He had been able for months to deal with such situations by searching and finding what was lost on his own or by calling for aid. But now the act of finding "for real" was assimilated to the old play format. Searching in earnest, he called out *allu down dere*, followed by "effort" sounds that he used in calling for aid (see Chapter 5). Having succeeded at that, albeit with the help of the experimenter, he then reverted to the play format. He now hid pencils *intentionally* behind the sofa cushions where before they had gone accidentally, greeting their retrieval by the experimenter or himself with his call of *allu*.

Richard and his mother, then, like Jonathan and his, gradually established a ritualized game in which they shared interchangeable roles. The game diversified and provided a place for the child's increasing initiative, as he learned both how to initiate the game and how to execute the moves. Both children learned easily how to keep the deep structure of the game constant while varying the surface structure. And both children managed before they were done to relate the game format to broader, more inclusive formats. The game provided a special occasion, free of pressure, to try out variations on the theme of appearance and disappearance. But in doing so, it also provided an opportunity for the child to participate in the establishment of the sorts of social convention upon which language use is based.

One final point before we bring our excursion into peekaboo to a close. It has to do with what before I called the Language Acquisition Support System. The peekaboo games of both children were replete with transitions in which mother would introduce a new procedure and gradually "hand it over" to the child as his skills for executing it developed. It is at the heart of any support system involving games—"play" games and language games alike. If the "teacher" in such a system were to have a motto, it would surely be "where before there was a spectator, let there now be a participant." One sets the game, provides a scaffold to assure that the child's ineptitudes can be rescued or rectified by appropriate intervention, and then removes the scaffold part by part as the reciprocal structure can stand on its own.

This "handover principle" is so ubiquitous that we hardly notice its presence. We will see its operation in the following chapters in the child's acquisition of reference and request. But it begins as early as the first interactions. Daniel Stern's work on the build-up of "turn taking" and "attunement" of mother and child, Kaye and Charney's study of how "turnarounds" in early exchanges are scaffolded by the mother until the child can take his own part in them, Brazelton's account of the mother and child's mutual interaction adjustments—all of these point to the same process of "setting up" the situation to make the child's entry easy and successful and then gradually pulling back and handing the role to the child as he becomes skillful enough to manage it.

Indeed, early in our research with Jonathan and Richard, I had become aware of this pattern when analyzing the structure of "give-and-take" games. Shortly after Richard reached his first birthday, we went back over the tapes to determine three things: (a) when he became the "hander-over" or agent in these games; (b) when he began to recognize that the aim of exchanging an object was not its possession, but the exchange itself; and (c) when he actually initiated give-and-take games. To get at the second of these, we simply timed how long he held an object in his possession before handing it back for exchange. The others were simply matters of counting.

The data are in the three figures below. Between five and nine months, the mother kept the exchange going. At nine months Richard "took off." After a long priming he moved swiftly into the role of agent, initiated games about half the time, and picked up the idea that you hand back an object, not hold on to it.

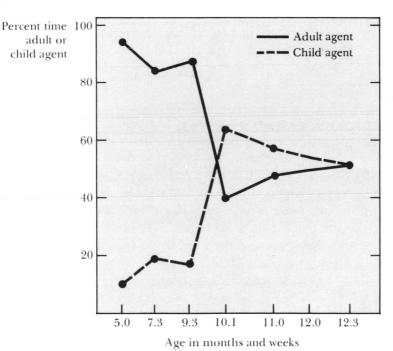

Age in months and weeks

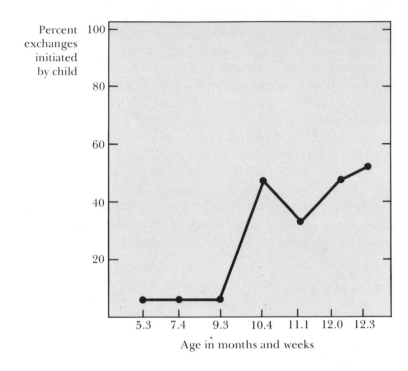

Percent exchanges initiated by child

Age in months and weeks

I apologize for the detail in which these simple games have been recounted. But the details highlight the general points with which the chapter opened. They do indeed, each of them, create a highly structured constitutive reality, a Wittgensteinian "form of life" on which the child learns to concentrate in a sequentially ordered manner while keeping the overall "logical" structures of the game in mind. The constitutive reality is first accompanied by vocalization and then anticipated by it. These vocalizations provide a skeletal or formal structure into which rich and more languagelike variants can later be introduced. They also provide a vehicle for practicing interchangeability of roles and for negotiating agency and other of the arguments of action. And they provide a unique opportunity for the child to shift from "natural" to conventional means of mediating the action.

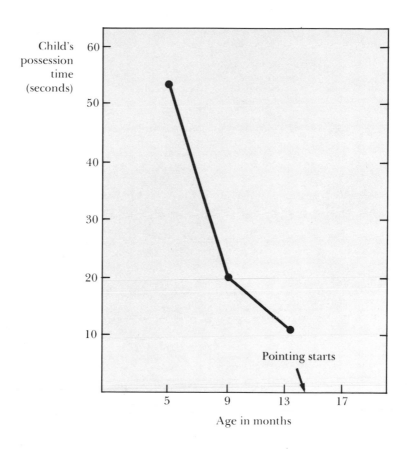

In the chapters that follow I propose to show how these same gamelike structures are imposed on such "bread-and-butter" formats as indicating and requesting—indeed, are essential to the development and elaboration of these communicative functions. They provide the vehicle that makes possible their conventionalization and, finally, their transformation from formats into more flexible and movable speech acts.

To this we turn next.

FOUR

The Growth of
Reference

THE AIM OF THIS CHAPTER is to explore some of the steps toward the mastery of linguistic reference. But before plunging into that task, we would be well advised to pause over the thornier complexities of that ancient topic.

It is, to begin with, impossible to proceed to an empirical study of reference without adopting a philosophical view with regard both to a philosophy of mind and a philosophy of language. Neutrality creates muddle. Yet this is not the place to review the empirical fruitfulness of contending philosophical views. I shall content myself simply by exposing my biases so that the reader may be forewarned.

The general or philosophical theory of reference that I have found most compatible with my own search for the psychological roots of reference is one put forward by Hilary Putnam. For my interest, like his, is in the causal historical chain that links an *introducing referential event* (when one person tries to indicate, however crudely, what he has on his mind) and some later *referential episode* (when each member of a communicating pair assigns a referential interpretation to a message that passes between them). This framework presupposes four things. The first is that individuals can signal to each other that they have a referential or indicating *intent*. The second is that reference can *vary* in precision from a rather woolly vagueness to a proper singular, definite referring expression. Indeed, two parties to a conversation may refer to the "same" topic with widely different degrees of precision. The "electricity" that a physicist mother has in mind will not be the "same" as what her child comprehends when she warns him about getting a shock. Still the two may carry on about "electricity" in spite of this indefiniteness. Their conversational negotiation may even *increase* her child's definiteness. Truth is not all that is involved in such causal chains. The child's conception of electricity may be vacuous or even wrong, yet there is a joint referent that not only exists in such asymmetric conversations, but that can be developed both for its truth value and its definiteness.

A third presupposition is that reference is a form of social interaction having to do with the management of *joint attention.* It is not simply a relation between something in one person's head and something in the world, as in the classical "reference triangle" of Ogden and Richards. It is characterized, rather, by a division of labor. In our example, one member of the pair may know all about electricity, the other only enough to have a placeholder for further specification. That is enough for an initial interaction.

The fourth and final presupposition of Putnam's position is that there is a goal-structure in referring. It is sustained not only by intent to refer, but by appropriate means for doing so and by specification as to when one has succeeded. The means comprise the set of procedures by which two people establish "jointness" in their attention. They vary from such evolved linguistic devices as anaphora (referring back to text) and deixis (referring back to context) to simple ostensive pointing. Achieving the *goal* of referring has little to do with agreement about a singular definite referent. It is enough that the parties to a referential exchange know they share enough overlap in their focal attention to make it worthwhile continuing, as Werner Deutsch and Tom Pechmann have noted. When the physicist mother tells her four-year-old that he has just been shocked by "electricity," she does not and need not assume that he has either the same extension or intension of the concept as she does. Nor need she care, if the conversation can only continue.

The problem of how reference develops can, accordingly, be restated as the problem of how people manage and direct each other's attention by linguistic means. We may properly ask how *linguistic* attention-management is superimposed on prelinguistic means and inquire as to how the first extends and modifies the second.

If we make the reasonable assumption that at some point the

child begins to develop some primitive notion of semanticity—
that patterned sounds stand for particular things or classes of
things in experience—then it is no great mystery that such sounds
will at first accompany ostensive referential gestures and eventually even replace them. The child may even initially use nonstandard but interpretable sound patterns that, in the interest of
keeping the negotiation of attention going, the adult comes to
imitate. But the linguistic community can be counted on to move
the language learner toward the standard forms of reference or
toward forms accessible to the community. Linguistic conventions and standard forms do not leap full grown from the egg.
They usually are slow transformations of initially primitive or
"natural " procedures that become socialized in negotiation.

Bringing another's attention to a joint focus is widespread in
the primate order. Michael Chance, describing the hierarchial
ordering of Old World monkeys, notes that even dominance
position can be defined by the distribution of attention in the
group—less dominant animals attending up the hierarchy, more
dominant ones being freer to extend their attention elsewhere.
Dominant animals force attention on themselves. Chimpanzees
in the wild and probably other Great Apes habitually follow the
line of regard of animals to determine the "target" of the others'
search. It is not plain whether they ever solicit or proffer information about a referent. What is unique about man, of course,
is that he manages joint attention by just such soliciting and pro-
ferring through the medium of indexes, icons, and symbols. It
is not surprising that six-month-old human infants, given their
primate inheritance, redirect their attention by following another's line of regard. What *is* surprising is that even during their
first year, they begin redirecting their attention in response to
subtle conventional cues that are features of adult language, such
as characteristic upward changes in intonation. The putative
referential system seems to be a very "open" one. It shifts very
easily from "natural" to "conventional" cues.

There is a key feature of human referring acts about which
nothing has been said thus far. They are highly context sensitive
or deictic. Parties to a referring act infer its referent from an

utterance in a *context*. Any account of the ontogenesis of reference must take this deictic feature into account. Indeed, John Lyons argues that deixis is the source of reference, that "locating in context" rather than simply "tagging" is the heart of reference, whether in early communication or later.

One might reasonably expect to find, then, that the acquisition of referring procedures is heavily dependent on the "arranging" and simplifying of contexts by the adult to assure that deictic demands be manageable for the child. Routinization of contexts would assure familiar, easily interpretable settings in which mother and child could locate or "place" objects and events to which they referred. The fact that the child already knows how to manage and interchange roles will, moreover, be of great help to him in relating his own referential acts to the acts of his partners in dialogue. For context and deixis depend on being able to shift and exchange perspective. The kinds of "game" skills discussed in the preceding chapter, including skill in negotiating turns and conditions, are crucial to referential activity—as we shall shortly see.

We turn now to how a mother and child in a highly reciprocal *interaction* attempt over the better part of a year to reach agreement (be it only a Putnam-like, partial overlap agreement) about what a thing shall be called.

The Management of Joint Attention

First steps take place early. As Robson and others since have noted, the earliest and most primitive phase of joint attention is the establishment of sustained eye-to-eye contact. Its beginning is an important milestone for the mother. It is the point when the mother often reports that her child has become a "real human being." It provokes much vocalization from the mother and, shortly after, from the child. By the end of the second month, eye-to-eye contact with vocal accompaniments has become well established. Mother and child begin to show turn taking in "turning on" and "turning off." Nobody has described this joining process better than Daniel Stern.

Our studies began after the turn taking and "communing" routines described by Stern had become established. We began when, at a second stage, the mother had begun introducing objects between the child and herself as targets for joint attention. In the case of Jonathan at three months, his mother introduced objects in two ways. One was by interposing the object between Jonathan and herself while the two were in eye-to-eye contact. As she does so, she changes her expression to a characteristic and standard form:

See the pretty dolly*

She characteristically accompanied the vocalization by moving the object into the child's line of regard and shaking or otherwise "forefronting" it. Her second approach was to pick up an object the child had already focused upon and to move it into the space between herself and the child, again shaking or looming it in as she vocalized.

Table 4.1 presents a sample of such object-play formats, some 303 in all for the two children. It records the number of instances of object highlighting and the number of discrete utterances.

Object highlighting is plainly a fixture of the early months. By the end of the first year it has virtually dropped out. With respect to accompanying utterances by the mothers, it is striking that they are *most* frequent during precisely those months when the two infants show *least* sign either of understanding or of producing language. Once language appears, the frequency begins to drop—although in Jonathan's case, it rises again, though with a quite different pattern and content, as we shall see. The "implicit" lesson being offered in these early object-play formats is that language accompanies attending to and handling objects— and in a way is phased to the actions in progress. Vocalization at this stage is a "place-holder" for later language that will be used when objects are being handled.

*The line superimposed on the utterance is an approximation of the stress in the mother's intonation.

Table 4.1 • OBJECT HIGHLIGHTING AND DISCRETE UTTERANCES
IN OBJECT-PLAY FORMATS BY THE CHILDREN'S MOTHERS

	Jonathan			*Richard*			
	Age in months			*Age in months*			
	3–9	*10–16*	*17–18*	*6–12*	*13–16*	*17–19*	*21–23*
Instances of highlighting	124	15	—	75	1	1	—
Highlightings per episode	2.03	0.29	—	0.82	0.03	0.06	—
Discrete utterances	704	253	130	830	186	65	100
Utterances per episode	11.5	4.87	8.12	9.02	4.76	4.06	3.85
Number of episodes	62	52	16	92	39	16	26

Once the children showed a reliable, readily evoked orient-
ing reaction to objects presented in this way, each mother
developed a characteristic, routinized way of preparing for
presentation when the child was *not* in eye-to-eye contact with
her. This took the form of an individually standardized attentional vocative based on the child's name.

By five months such vocatives had become workaday means for
getting the child to look toward the mother or to search for an
attentional target.

"Proper name" vocatives were soon after expanded by addi-
tions of the following kind:

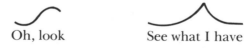

John Lyons, in his discussion of Quasi-English as a developmental "starting language," speaks of such attentional vocatives as

"undifferentiated deictics" that specify that there is something somewhere in the environment to attend to. By the end of the first year these expressions become general alerting signals to the child about the possibility of a shift in attention focus.

Here the work of Maire Logan Ryan is particularly relevant. She worked with mother-baby pairs, infants aged twelve months, whose mothers were all native speakers of Glaswegian English. These mothers, she found, were much more likely to use a rising intonation pattern when shifting reference to something other than what their children were attending to. A second, associated finding was more striking: A baby was more likely to change the focus of her attention to the object that her mother was holding when the mother spoke with a rising intonation pattern than when she did not. Current work on the responsiveness of children to such undifferentiated deictic intonational cues suggests that the fast-rising stress may have a "natural" power to attract an infant's attention.

The first phase of managing joint attention, very much under the control of the mother, thus appears to result in the child discovering signals in the mother's speech that indicate that the *mother* is attending to "something to look at." Seven months seemed to be the age at which our children reached sensitivity to "undifferentiated deictics."

A concomitant phase in development is more specific and relates to the child being able better to spot *what* it is that occupies another's attention. In its simplest form, it consists of the child's following another's line of regard to a target at a distance from the two of them. Michael Scaife and I did the first simple experiment, involving an adult sitting opposite an infant (subjects ranging from three months to somewhat over a year), first making eye-to-eye contact and then turning ninety degrees either to left or right and looking outward intently. The turn was accompanied by a stressed "oh, look." By eight to ten months, two-thirds of our infants were following the shifted line of regard, and by one year all of them were. The experiment was done more carefully by Butterworth, and he noted several additional features in the gaze-following pattern. The first and most

important was that the one-year-old child would look out along
the line of regard, search for an object, and if he found none,
would return to the adult's face for a second look, following which
he would turn outward again. There seemed to be an expectancy that a target could be found. The second feature was that
the infant would not turn outward a greater angular distance in
search of the object than the point at which he still held the adult's
face in the periphery of his gaze. In effect, he was looking for
an object, but doing so while keeping the adult in his visual field.
The concurrent search for a target and the maintaining of contact suggest that we are indeed dealing with a very much more
specific form of attention management than that provided by
the undifferentiated deictic. Unfortunately, this type of more
specific deictic marking of a putative referent has not been
experimentally combined with the nonspecific attentional vocative discussed earlier, but we did note informally that the likeli-
hood of a child following gaze direction increased when the
experimenter's turned gaze was accompanied by some such
expression as "oh, look."

I must digress for a moment to comment on the seeming
departure from egocentrism these infants showed. After all, they
were able to "take another's perspective" in searching the environment. Doubtless there are many respects in which infants and
young children are egocentric in the sense Piaget and others have
intended, but I think it is necessary to recognize that there is an
important countervailing tendency operative. The briefest way
of characterizing it is to say that infants and young children from
very early on appear, like adults, to be Naïve Realists who believe
that there is a world of objects "out there" and that others are
experiencing the same world that they are. And, indeed, whatever philosophical position we adults may eventually take, however constructionalist our epistemology may become, I think
Naïve Realism is everybody's working belief—a point that has
been made with some philosophical force by Hilary Putnam and
argued psychologically by William Hogan.

By the sixth or seventh month, the child's attention becomes dominated by his efforts to reach and take objects, to exchange them, and so on. We shall speak of this later in connection with the growth of request. Here it suffices to say only that joint attention, in the months after reaching is well developed, becomes dominated by joint action while the child develops the kinds of "action schemas" and scripts about the world that were discussed earlier. The principal achievement during this active phase is that the child now becomes a *giver* of signals about objects desired and is not just involved in comprehending and decoding others' efforts to direct his attention.

A crucial next phase begins with the emergence of pointing by the child. "Pure" pointing, so-called, emerged at nine and a half months in Jonathan and at thirteen months in Richard. The difference in ages may have had to do with the earlier age at which Richard began walking. Jonathan, a "slow walker," required a signaling system to the objects he could not get to easily. Pointing does not appear to be an extension or modification of reaching, even of ostensive or conventionalized reaching of that effortless kind by which the child (as we shall see) indicates an object that he wishes to be obtained for him without quite reaching for it. It seems more likely that pointing is part of a primitive marking system for singling out the noteworthy. Obviously, the child has been exposed to pointing by adults, and his ability to comprehend an adult point precedes his own production by a month or two in our records. In Jonathan's case the first observed points are toward near-distant objects seen through the garden window, his point sometimes being accompanied by a protodemonstrative *um*. Richard's first points (sometimes accompanied by *da*) are for old objects seen in new contexts (cup that mother has put on her head) and for new objects in familiar contexts (as when magpies fly into the field next to his summer cottage). Pictures also evoke pointing—familiar pictures particularly, when seen in a book. Pointing, it appears, also occurs in efforts to give "abstract" or uncertain referents a locus. I must say a word about a concurrent development before I can suggest what this last development might mean.

I refer to the concurrent appearance of phonetically consistent but nonstandard expressions by which the child comes to "indicate" objects. It appears to be the start of a genuine semanticity hypothesis—that particular, non standard voiced sounds indicate particular classes of objects. These voiced sounds took the place of the demonstratives *da* and *um*. In any case, Richard had by this time begun to produce such forms modeled loosely on adult speech, e.g., *apoo* for apple, *boe* for bird, etc.

It was in connection with *boe* that we observed pointing as a rather "abstract" locative act. Richard had (as earlier noted) been observing rooks and magpies (new to him) flying about that afternoon in a field next to the summer cottage in which he was staying. That evening when he was indoors, seated on the floor, fortunately being videorecorded, he sat quietly for some moments, then pointing upward he uttered (rather absently and tentatively) his word for "bird," *boe*. He seemed to be locating in his "present" space an object recalled from memory. His lexeme, *boe,* served as a nominal specifier of his point with a spatial deictic in the absence of an actual object. Magda Kalmar has observed and photographed a similar phenomenon in which a child, in much the same stage of development as Richard, is listening to a clock held to his ear. He seems puzzled as to where the sound is coming from. Finally, he points upward as he listens, as if giving the sound a spatial context.

Let me briefly comment on the referential specificity of phonetically consistent forms. *Boe* was quite specific. Its semantic scope was limited to flying birds. But take Richard's *ghee*. He seemed to use it in much the same way as one might use an expression like *thingumabob*. *Ghee* referred either to "new" objects that were impressive in appearance but small in size or to familiar objects for which he knew no name or to objects that were somewhat surprising in context—uses similar to those discussed earlier for pointing. *Ghee* was used rather like a placeholder for "name-worthy" objects.

Once pointing and phonetically consistent forms appear, they are very soon recruited into the familiar "Where" and "What" games that had long before been established. Jonathan's mother began her *Where's the X? Where did it go?* as early as four months, and Richard's started her *What's this?* for presenting objects at nine months—in neither case with any possibility of appropriate response. But once pointing appears, *Where's the X?* becomes a *real* request for a point. This routine is well established for Jonathan by twelve months and for Richard by thirteen to fourteen months.

At fifteen months, this query is incorporated by the parents of both children into the formatted game of "Body Parts." *Where's your nose?*, etc. (answered by an appropriate point) is soon followed by *What's that?* (mother pointing to the child's nose). *What's that?*, of course, evokes vocalizations, then nonstandard lexemes, and finally names.

What's that? and *Where's the X?* go hand in glove. They are classic instances of indexicals—in the sense of relating a sign to an element of immediate nonlinguistic context. The child's mastery of such indexicals now makes possible the development of new discourse patterns that permit movement to a more advanced level of dealing intralinguistically with language—words relating to other words and not simply to elements of nonlinguistic context. To that we turn next.

"Book Reading": The Growth of Discourse Labels

Anat Ninio and I kept a particular watch on Richard and his mother "reading books" during the course of Richard's second year. It was one of Richard's favorite games, and we simply made video recordings of its natural occurrence without having to request any "performances." It seemed like a particularly good window through which to observe not only how naming was managed, but also to observe descriptions of action—all in the context of discourse and dialogue. The books, of course, were "picture books." Earlier forms of this kind of "dialogue" were about body parts or about things, the names of concrete objects serving as topics. Those earlier forms also took on a gamelike format as in give-and-take and the kinds of exchanges described in the preceding chapter. Those games, recall, impose roles, turn taking, joint attention, and a sequential structure. Book reading is built on those already established skills. But now there is exchange about nonconcrete, pictured topics. The previously established skills, like turn taking, are virtually perfect right from the start of book reading. Only about 1 percent of the two participants' utterances, for example, occur simultaneously rather than alternately.

Throughout, the mother tailors her participation in book reading to the child's apparent competence. It is hard to know how "conscious" she is of what she is doing, for this matching is so automatic—even when four-year-olds talk to younger children, as Rochelle Gelman and Marilyn Shatz have so elegantly shown.

The variety of the mother's utterance types in book reading is strikingly limited. She makes repeated use of four key utterance types, with a surprisingly small number of variant tokens of each. These types were (1) the Attentional Vocative, e.g., *Look;* (2) the Query, e.g., *What's that?;* (3) the Label, e.g., *It's an X;* and (4) the Feedback Utterance, e.g., *Yes.* They are illustrated below by an example from a session at 1;1.1.

MOTHER: Look! (Attentional Vocative)
  CHILD: (Touches picture)
MOTHER: What are those? (Query)
  CHILD: (Vocalizes a babble string and smiles)
MOTHER: Yes, they are rabbits. (Feedback and Label)
  CHILD: (Vocalizes, smiles, and looks up at mother)
MOTHER: (Laughs) Yes, rabbit. (Feedback and Label)
  CHILD: (Vocalizes, smiles)
MOTHER: Yes. (Laughs) (Feedback)

Table 4.2 contains the distribution of each of the four utterance types and their tokens.

The four utterance types and their tokens account for virtually all of the mother's utterances in the "reading format" for

Table 4.2 • UTTERANCES CLASSIFIED AS TOKENS OF
THE FOUR MAJOR TYPES OF THE MOTHER'S SPEECH

Type / Tokens	Frequency
I. Attentional Vocatives	**65**
Look!	61
Look at that!	4
II. Query	**85**
What's that?	57
What are those?	8
What are they doing?	6
What is it?	5
What are they?	1
What's on that page?	1
What have we got here?	1
What's the next one?	1
What's over here?	1
What else can you see there?	1
What does that do?	1
What do you see there?	1
What can you see?	1
III. Label	**216**
X (= a stressed label)	91
It's an X	34
That's an X	28
There is an X	12
An X	12
That's X	6
There is X	6
Lots of X	5
They are X-ing . . . (e.g., going to bed)	5
More X	3
They are X	3
These are the X	3
The X	2
You can see the X	1
That one is an X	1
Look at the X	1
It says: X	1
We'll call it an X	1
Kind of X	1

Table 4.2 (continued)

Type / Tokens	Frequency
IV. Feedback	**80**
Yes	50
Yes, I know	8
It's not an X	5
That's it!	3
Isn't it?	2
Not X	2
No, it's not X	2
Yes, it is	1
That's charming	1
You are right	1
No, it's an X, not a Y	1
No, it's an X	1
Yes, they are	1
Yes, very good	1
That's not an X	1

the whole of the period studied. For each of the types, a *single* token accounts for from nearly half to more than 90 percent of the instances. Moreover, the intonation of these utterances is virtually unchanged from the early to the late sessions (with a few exceptions to be noted later).

The key utterance types, moreover, were governed by strict discourse and ordering constraints. Within a given cycle, the order of utterances was remarkably stable. They occur almost exclusively in the order:

(1) Attentional Vocative
(2) Query
(3) Label
(4) Feedback

Variations are almost always in the form of a deletion of an element. One or two steps may be left out for reasons that will be plain in a moment. In short, if an Attentional Vocative occurs it will almost surely be the first utterance; if a Query occurs it will be before a Label or Feedback. In consequence, the four utterance types form an ordered Guttman scale of over 85 percent reproducibility, far in excess of chance.

When a step is left out, it is for good reason, as noted. Richard's mother responds to what he does. If *he* initiates a cycle by pointing or vocalizing, she responds with a Query and omits the Attentional Vocative. Or, if he offers an acceptable label after her Query, she will virtually always skip the Label and jump to Feedback. In a word, she is responding to him as she would to a "real" partner in an exchange. That premise provides the basic structure of their format.

Table 4.3 • DISTRIBUTION OF MOTHER'S AND CHILD'S
LABELS BY REFERENTIAL FOCUS

Type of Referent	Percent of Mother's Labels	Percent of Child's Labels
Common nouns of whole objects	88.9	89.8
Common nouns of parts of objects	2.9	4.1
Proper names	4.1	4.1
Other (actions, attributes, etc.)	4.1	2.0
Total percent	100.0	100.0
Total number of labels	170	49

The mother bypasses the Wittgensteinian dilemma ("What feature of a referent does a label refer to?"). Nearly 90 percent of her labels refer to *whole objects* (see Table 4.3), and since half of the remainder are made up of proper names that also stand for the whole, she creates few difficulties about feature extraction. If, as both Willard Quine and Itzak Schlesinger propose, language learners are "body-minded" rather than "feature-minded," Richard's mother is on their side. Body-mindedness may not solve *all* of Wittgenstein's dilemmas, but it seems to bypass this one. For there were virtually no confusions as to what Richard's mother's labels referred.

In responding to Richard's efforts, his mother appeared to

be operating on a freshly updated, detailed "inventory" of his knowledge of objects and events, of the words he had previously understood, and of the forms of expression of which he was capable. In the main, she gave him the benefit of the doubt when he made an ambiguous utterance (of which more presently) or "excused" a wrong response to her Query with kind words and expression. *You haven't seen one of those; that's a goose.* Or *You don't really know what those are, do you? They are mittens; wrong time of the year for those.* Or *It's a dog; I know you know that one. We'll find you something you know very well.* But she could also insist: *Come on, you've learned 'bricks.'* On the whole, as with the games reported in the preceding chapter, the mother created an accepting and supporting situation. Exceptions to this rule (like exceptions to Grice's maxims of conversation) were reasoned ones whose function we will presently examine.

Table 4.4 sets out the rate and nature of Richard's participation in book reading. His active responses included vocaliza-

Table 4.4 • PROPORTION OF READING CYCLES IN WHICH THE CHILD MADE ACTIVE RESPONSES

Age	Number of Reading Cycles	Percent of Cycles in Which Child Made at Least One Active Response	Number of Active Turns by the Child	Percent of Active Turns Containing a Vocalization	Percent of Vocalizations That are Lexical Labels
0;8.14	2	50.0	4	0.0	0.0
0;11.7	9	55.6	17	35.3	0.0
1;0.25	7	71.4	10	90.0	0.0
1;1.7	6	83.3	13	76.9	0.0
1;1.22	40	37.5	17	41.2	0.0
1;2.7	26	43.8	18	38.9	28.6
1;3.13	36	86.1	60	93.3	50.0
1;3.21	18	88.9	22	95.4	61.9
1;4.14	35	77.1	50	92.0	54.3
1;5.8	19	80.2	32	100.0	28.1
1;5.22	4	100.0	5	100.0	20.0
1;6.1	7	100.0	12	100.0	50.0

tion, gesture, smile, eye contact with mother, and search for a specified object. Note that, not surprisingly, participation increases steadily with age. And obviously he vocalizes more and his vocalizations become more interpretable at the same time.

The appearance of some standard lexical labels at 1;2 encouraged Richard's mother to believe that he had mastered the "semanticity hypothesis"—that he knew now that sounds have meanings. She began to act as if her child were capable of words rather than mere babbles. Her "imputation rules" for the child's vocalizations changed sharply. Now she treated them as if they "meant" something or, when they were ambiguous, as if they *should* mean something. In the latter case, if she could not make out what they meant, she pressed him to repeat or to repair his utterance. She became much firmer in her demands, though still permissive in her interpretations.

After the appearance of those first lexeme-length phonologically constant babbles, she treated his babbling in a new way. Whereas before she accepted his babbling efforts permissively, as if they were *attempts* at labeling to which she supplied a corrective label, now she demanded that he respond more lexically. She would repeat the *What's that?* Query, often with the tag *You know, don't you?* She still maintained the order of utterance types described earlier, but now she would repeat one of them, the Query, until Richard gave a satisfactory performance. A shorter, lexeme-length babble would do. She had plainly upped her requirements.

Once the child was plainly capable of producing words, or wordlike sounds, his mother raised the ante again. Just as before she would not accept incoherent long babbles but only lexeme-length ones, now she insisted on words. Even then, she remained tuned to his capacities and would avoid pressing him too hard. The game remained a game. There were few confrontations.

A crucial step occurred in the labeling game when the mother knew that Richard knew the label she was asking for. Now she began to use a sharply different intonation pattern in her Query to signal that "I know that you know." Her *What's that?* Query was now given with a falling intonation when she asked about words that (in her estimate) the child already knew. Mother and child were on to the presuppositional distinction between the *given* and the *new*. When the presuppositionally marked Query was given with a falling intonation contour, Richard looked knowingly at his mother and smiled and might even "tease" her by delaying response a bit.

Wallace Chafe makes the interesting point that the distinction between old and new information is closely akin to that between topic and comment or subject and predicate. And it is of more than passing interest that the old or established labels were the ones around which the mother began elaborating comments and questions for new information, such as,

MOTHER: What's that? (falling intonation)
  CHILD: Fishy.
MOTHER: Yes, and what's he doing?

Now the rising intonation is shifted to "doing" in her final turn— as if a predicate of action (something new) is being called for. And soon the game shifted from labeling to predication.

What psychological "engine" drives the child's mastery of labeling? Is it, as Saint Augustine would have us believe, some sort of imitation? Obviously, there must be some imitative element, but it is certainly not "direct" imitation. The evidence is against it. Take first the child's repetition of a label provided by his mother at the appropriate place in the cycle. He repeats it about half the time. But this rate of repetition is no higher than that which occurs when *he* himself provides the label as a response to his mother's Query and then repeats himself. He also repeats about half the time after his mother's feedback or after her repetition of his label. Looked at another way, we can ask whether he is more impelled to reply to a Query that asks for a label or to repeat a label just uttered by his mother. *What's that?* produces eight times as many labeling responses as imitations of his mother's label. The child is trying to answer a question. The mother's label provides him with a model for doing so. But the model word is to be used in *reply to a question*—not as an imitation of the parent. He, the child, is responding to the *intent* of his mother's question. He rarely mirrors her label.

How did he come to understand that intent? That intuition preceded by months the beginning of the book-reading format. Its "origin" is probably "natural," whatever that means. Like gaze following or "point following," both also "natural," appreciation of Query intent is soon incorporated by the mother into a conventionalized format that permits the introduction of signs, anticipations, and the like. The mother in all these cases conventionalizes her signaling of "intentions," "objects," and "events" as fast as the child can manage "uptake" of her conventions. She then moves on and embeds these newly established skills into still newer routines, raising the ante when she judges the child to be ready.

At each step in this progression, she is establishing a placeholder at which more symbolic routines can be substituted later. Undifferentiated deictics are replaced by pointing. Undifferentiated babbles in response to Queries in the book-reading format are first replaced by lexeme-length babbles and then by words.

One is led to conclude that as the infant masters the routines of one level, enough processing capacity is freed for him to manage the next step forward, as Marilyn Shatz has suggested. What permits this requisite freeing to occur, of course, is the opportunity to use and thus perfect communicative routines in mother-steadied, formatted dialogue. If you should now ask what leads the child to take his steps forward, why he does not stay at the level where he was, then we shall have to speculate about the operation of a Language Acquisition Device or of some more general push to competence. It is obviously not sufficient to say only that the child has more processing capacity "freed up" by his increased mastery. There must also be some push that moves him toward more evolved linguistic performance as well. What that is remains as mysterious as before. But that the mother and the adult world provide a steadying support system for that growth is plain enough. What we have seen is that over this crucial period in the growth of reference, the mother remains steady in her principled responses to the child's efforts, changing only enough to take account of his emerging skill, promoting it and pushing it lightly. She remains steady, so to speak, so that the child can try out and consolidate his changes.

Theory Revisited

Several issues raised at the start of the chapter can now profit by being visited again.

Recall Putnam's discussion of asymmetry in reference, as with the physicist mother warning her child about electricity. I think the example we have explored—Richard and his mother dealing with reference—underlines his point. Their interchange seems to be governed by the principle that no speaker is *entirely* ignorant—an extension of his Principle of Reasonable Ignorance, which asserts that no speaker is entirely omniscient. We operate with the belief that any topic can be referred to (or brought to the attention of) anybody by some means that will be comprehensible to them. It is the ground principle, I think, upon which reference is negotiated.

Mothers' early indicating and "reference teaching" is precisely of this order. They often do not know what their children have in mind when they vocalize or gesture, nor are they sure their own speech has been understood by their children. But they are prepared to negotiate in the tacit belief that *something* comprehensible can be established. Take the following example from Richard's book reading at twenty-three months.

MOTHER: What's that?
  CHILD: Ouse.
MOTHER: Mouse, yes. That's a mouse.
  CHILD: More mouse (pointing to another picture).
MOTHER: No, those are squirrels. They're like mice but with long tails. Sort of.
  CHILD: Mouse, mouse, mouse.
MOTHER: Yes, all right, they're mice.
  CHILD: Mice, mice.

On later occasions, doubtless, the negotiations will continue and Richard will eventually settle on a reasonable referential handling of rats and squirrels much as, for example, the subjects in the experiment by Susan Carey and Elsa Bartlett settle down to a reasonable way of handling *Chromium* after negotiating their alternative hypotheses about what color it might stand for. Children depend upon such corrective possibilities in the linguistic community they have entered. It starts early, as we have seen, and it can become strikingly complicated very early.

Take this example at twenty-two months. Richard is trying out the semantic scope of a word in the hope of finding where the boundaries can be drawn. He and his mother are examining an English penny together.

RICHARD: (Points to picture of the Queen on coin) Nanny, nanny.

MOTHER: What? That's not Granny. It's a lady, yes. Nini is a lady, isn't it?

RICHARD: (Points to coin again) Nanny, nanny.

MOTHER: You think that's Granny? Oh well, I don't think she'd mind too much.

RICHARD: Layly (with smile to mother).

MOTHER: Queen.

RICHARD: Nanny, nanny.

MOTHER: It's *not*.

RICHARD: Nini (smiles and nods).

MOTHER: Yes.

RICHARD: (Points and says) Nini.

MOTHER: Have they all got ladies on?

RICHARD: Nanny, nanny (points).

MOTHER: No, it isn't.

RICHARD: Nini.

And so he is on his way to distinguishing Granny from the Queen and both from generic ladies. Note that this negotiation has been going on for a long while. At eighteen months, *nini* and *nanny* were both indicators for juice. At twenty months, *eeni* was for lemon and *nana* was used to indicate "nothing there" when something was expected. At the time of this example, *nani* may be money and *nini* lady, and there is much sorting still to be done. By twenty-three months, for example, *nini* disappears, and at twenty-four months, Richard says, *There's a lady.*

One can conclude, I think, that the achievement of reference by the child depends upon his mastery of discourse and dialogue rules as much as upon his individual skills at linking percepts with sounds and with representations of the world in his head. For reference is dependent, as we have seen, not only upon mastering a relationship between sign and significate, but upon using social procedures in concert with one another to assure that the sign and the significate that become linked overlap in some negotiable way with the uses of others. The starting paradigm for all of this is the achievement of joint attention, but as we have seen with our subject, Richard, by the time a couple of years have passed, he is calibrating his joint attention not on "natural" objects in the perceptual world, but on such matters as whether the Queen, his grandmother, and ladies in general shall be brought to attention by one or by several linguistic distinctions. What finally emerges is indeed the result of a historical process, as Hilary Putnam argues. John Lyons (as I mentioned earlier) once entitled an essay "Deixis as the Source of Reference." Doubtless he had a strong case. I think an equally strong case has been made in this chapter for the claim that discourse and dialogue are also the sources of reference. If they were not, each speaker would be locked in a web of isolated reference triangles of his own making—if indeed he could construct such a web on his own.

FIVE

The Development of Request

O F ALL FORMS OF LANGUAGE USE, requesting is bound to be the one most deeply enmeshed in context. Whether we request information, goods, services, or mere recognition, we must accommodate the hearer's capacities, his constraints, our relation to him, and the conventions to which he adheres both in language and in the real world. The object of request is to get somebody to deliver the goods. And the goods are in the real world, not only in language.

Requesting is, consequently, a rich topic in the study of pragmatics, and it has been studied with a variety of aims in view—for its underlying logic by Hintikka, for its grammatical forms by Jerrold Katz, and for its part in speech act theory by John Searle. But there is a surprising lack of work on the *acquisition* of acts of requesting, although we do know something about the child's acquisition of the syntactic inversion rules in the interrogative mode, or that a surprisingly large proportion of interrogatives are addressed to prelinguistic children or (more to our point) that very early on the young child is sensitive to the felicity conditions on request, as Garvey has shown.

Our object in this chapter, as in the last, is pragmatic: to explore the growth of requesting in our two young subjects, Richard and Jonathan. As with reference, requesting begins diffusely and "naturally," the child gesturing and vocalizing in a way that is interpretable, indicating *that* he is in want, but not indicating *what* he wants. In no sense are these "signs" conventional at the start: fretting, crying, reaching, etc. There is some evidence from the work of D. M. Ricks and others that the mother is able, when the child is three or four months old, to distinguish different kinds of cries—hunger, pain, etc. But in the main her correctness is attributable to the mother's skill in *interpreting* what the child "needs" rather than how he is vocalizing. Context is virtually all.

There are interesting developmental changes in the forms of inference that guide the mother's interpretations. Christopher Pratt in his Oxford thesis on the socialization of crying reports that up to about twenty-six weeks of age, an infant's cry is typically interpreted by his mother as indicating frustration, discomfort, hunger, or a wish to be picked up. The infant's needs are seen as "physical." Pratt finds, moreover, that before twenty-six weeks the child is in fact more likely to stop crying when the mother responds by ministering to these physical needs by feeding, resettling, or comforting the child. At about twenty-six weeks the mother begins interpreting the child's cries as due to more psychological "causes." And just around then, he is increasingly likely to respond to her "psychological" interventions: being offered an object, being engaged in "conversation," and the like.

The next real change occurs a few weeks later, at about eight months, when the child begins to show the first referentially interpretable indication of *what* he is requesting. By this time, his demand signaling has become quite socialized. It takes the form of a much more ritualized cry: less persistent, more punctuated by pauses during which the child checks on uptake by the mother or by other adults. Acoustically as well, his cries also become more "conventional," his initial "flat" sound spectrum being replaced by cries with a more pronounced fundamental frequency. The child's signaling of request progresses steadily toward conventionalization in this manner even before he can signal *what* he wants. The illocutionary aspects of request grow before the referential element is present. So long as the mother can provide an interpretation of an appropriate referent from context, the child adapts his cries to such felicity conditions as the mother imposes—prohibitions on "screaming," waiting for uptake, etc. But once the child is able to signal not only *that* he wants something, but *what* it is that he wants, conventionalization moves at a much more rapid pace.

The mother's accuracy and speed in interpreting what her

child wants obviously depends on his skills as well. But this progress is interesting. The point at which our two mothers began successfully to interpret referential intent in their sons' signaling was just about when we, as "onlookers," were able to do so. It has entirely to do with the child's first "requestive referential" maneuver: arm extension *toward* a desired object, occurring at about eight months in both children. At first, this reach is as if "real": it is effortful, the body is inclined with the reach, and the child makes "effortful" noises while opening and closing his extended hand. In a few months, this reach has become stylized and conventional. The reach is now open-handed, noneffortful, and its accompanying vocalization (as we shall see) becomes distinctive. It is, in effect, an "ostensive reach" that seems to be intended to indicate an object of desire. But it is *not* a point. It is only much later that the child combines a "pure point" with a request to indicate what he wants. Rather, it is a striking instance of a mode of indexing that is specifically tied to request.

We distinguish three main types of request in the two children. The first, and the simplest procedurally, is *request for an object*. Object request is elaborated from an early phase when it is directed exclusively to a present, close, and visible object often in possession of an adult who may be offering it to the child; to later forms directed to remote but visible objects out of reach; and finally to a form designed to request objects that are out of view.

I have called a second type *invitation*, for it is a request to an adult to share a *role relationship* in play or in a game. Such requests, obviously, are contextualized in highly familiar routines like object exchange and the games discussed in a preceding chapter.

A third type is a *request for supportive action* in which the child tries to recruit an adult's skill or strength to help him achieve a desired goal. These requests often require the child to have some knowledge of the structure of the task at hand, but this may not be so at the start. But supportive requests, as they become more specialized, depend as much upon the child's representation of tasks as they do upon his communicative competence. Invitations can take advantage of established game procedures; requests for supportive action require the child to combine his knowledge of a task with his knowledge of how to signal.

The mother's role differs in each type of request. In one, she must figure out what object the child wants; in another what the invitation is for; and in the third, what kind of help he needs. But in all three types of request, she has a common "teaching" function as well, however informal it may be. She is the "agent of the culture," so to speak, and it is she who enforces the felicity conditions on requesting—and, as we shall see, by a great deal of negotiation.

The incidence of the three types of request at different ages is set forth in Table 5.1.

Table 5.1 • PERCENTAGE OF REQUESTS OF DIFFERENT TYPES
MADE BY JONATHAN AND RICHARD AT VARIOUS AGES

| | *Child's Age in Months* | | | | | |
	8–10	11–12	13–14	15–16	17–18	20–24*
Requests for:			(*percentage*)			
Near and visible object	65	100	63	49	23	11
Remote or absent object	—	—	11	23	11	24
Joint role enactment	—	—	19	14	25	39
Supportive action	35†	—	7	14	41	26
Total number of requests	26	23	27	22	54	38
Minutes of recording	210	150	150	150	150	150
Number of requests made every 10 minutes	1.2	1.5	1.8	1.5	3.6	2.5

*Richard only
†Jonathan only

Object Request

The child's first requests for objects are usually reciprocals of adult offers: the mother holds out a toy invitingly, and the child reaches toward it, extending his arm as noted earlier, and the adult hands it over. From eight to fourteen months, of the fifty-seven nearby objects requested by the two children, forty-seven (82 percent) were in another's possession. The reaching was often accompanied by a fret or effort sound. First object requesting, then, appears to be a counterpart of "taking possession" of something possessed by another. Up to about nine months, the child's gaze is directed exclusively to the object he is requesting. Indeed, the two children only looked at their mothers' faces when they failed to take possession of the objects sought. Susan Sugarman has described the "object schema" of the child as initially being independent of his "mother schema." But it could not be completely so. Else why would he be tempted to request objects principally in her possession? Nor does he seize the held object straightaway. He gestures first, extending his hand *toward* the object and pausing. Only one instance of an outright grab was recorded (at eleven months) and that was when a desired object was held by another infant. This surely suggests that the child, even in this early period, recognizes request as a way of altering possession by indirect means. But it is true that it is only by nine months that the two children glance at their mothers concurrently with reaching for the object. Whether initially independent or not, the "object schema" and the "mother schema" do seem to become better coordinated with time.

Two things happen next. The first is that the child's reach for the object becomes converted into what I referred to earlier as a stylized or ostensive reach, without signs of effort or fretting. The accompanying effort sounds were concurrently replaced by stylized request calls: *huhmm* for Jonathan and *heaah* for Richard. The children, however, were still deficient in acknowledging receipt of the object when it was handed to them.

Glancing toward the mother on receipt occurred only one time in five until the sixteenth month. By that age, the children were quite regularly looking toward the mother's face both when they made their vocally accompanied ostensive reach and on receipt— so long as their "eagerness" was not excessive. More usually, they recognized the role of the mother as in possession and as due a request. If they were overeager, they regressed back to fretting and effortful reaching. In any case, the format of this more socialized variant of object-request was well established by eighteen months. And at that point it began to serve as a "carrier" for more speechlike forms.

At sixteen months, for example, Richard replaced his requestive *heaah* vocalization with an extraordinarily well articulated *ghee* of which mention was made in the preceding chapter. That in turn was replaced by sentencelike babble strings in the same privileged position, accompanying the ostensive, effortless reach, a favorite being *n-gah-gho-ah-di*. Shortly after eighteen months, these delightful, rather interrogatively contoured strings dropped out to be replaced in the same position by idiosyncratic lexemes like *bauble* (apple), accompanying a reach toward a book on the shelf containing a favorite picture of an apple. And indeed, by twenty months the ostensive reach was beginning to disappear, replaced by a new intonation pattern. *Heaah* or *ghee* now became the head word in an utterance containing an idiosyncratic lexeme in terminal position. The lexeme rather than the "request marker" received the stress—as in *Heaah moo-louse* ("Want the mouse") with the first syllable, *moo,* stressed. And not long after, at twenty-two months, *heaah* is dropped altogether and two-word combinations signifying Recurrence (*more mouse*) and Possession (*Richard cake*) make their appearance in the request format. In a word, grammatical forms and semantic relations are used in the same format to replace the invented forms used initially to signal both requestive intent and the object desired. The format was very much the steady vehicle of the development.

There seemed to be no evidence of any deliberate modeling by the mother of the grammatical forms that emerged in the children's speech. Correct grammatical forms, rather, were offered as disambiguating *interpretations* of the child's request: *Do you want more X? Is that what you want?* They were genuine, nonpedagogical efforts by the mother to figure out the child's utterance. Obviously, these utterances served as models, but they were not, so to speak, offered in advance to be imitated.

Pedagogy, rather, is reserved for making the child mind the preparatory, essential, sincerity, and affiliative conditions on making a request. Richard's mother, for example, is particularly eager from the start to insure the sincerity of his requests: *Do you really want it?* being one of her consistent utterances. She later became concerned with essential conditions on requesting—did Richard really need help or could he act on his own: *Come on, you can do it, come on;* or on one occasion, *Come on, make the ultimate effort.* By affiliative conditions I mean the child having to respect his mother as an ally rather than as an adversary: *Don't shout or I won't give it to you.*

There was a gentle pressure from the mother to get her child to use the advanced forms he had already shown himself capable of in earlier discourse. It was much the same as with growth of reference where the mother would not accept a less advanced form when she believed a higher form was in her child's range. She did not always accede and even scolded on occasion: *No, banging won't produce it* or *What's all that about? It's not very informative, you know.* Indeed, half of Richard's mother's responses to his object requests up to fourteen months include some effort to make him carry out the act on his own or to specify more clearly what he wanted. After that, she relaxed very considerably, but that was because he had become more requestively felicitous.

The request format underwent major elaboration midway through both children's second year. The change was produced by two new variants of requesting: requesting absent objects, and requesting assistance in carrying out some activity (of which more later). The first of these, of course, requires a degree of specification not needed when an object is within reach or sight. An object out of sight requires the use of nominals for easy specification. And nominals surged into use at this time. They were there before, but now they had a new function and the new function appeared to stimulate their further growth—and further teaching by the mother, mostly in supplying "words." This growth, of course, was concurrent with the developments described in the last chapter.

Another way of specifying a remote referent is by indicating not by name but by "canonical locus"—e.g., pointing to or even naming the icebox where some desired food is located. While this procedure depends upon contextual interpretation by the mother, it reduces uncertainty very considerably. If you have no name for an object, pointing to its usual location serves nicely. Both children used it as a standby until their lexicons were up to the range of objects they desired.

Remote or displaced requests began at the landmark age of fourteen months in both children. Curiously, canonical-locus indicating as its vehicle produced something of a regression in both children. An old form—reach-plus-vocalization—was fulfilling a new function—but not well. Ostensive reaches of this kind began involving the whole body again when they failed. Accompanying vocalizations became more prolonged, more insistent. For Richard, his typical *heeeaah* was stretched out though its falling intonation was retained. Jonathan imposed an undulating intonation on his prolonged *hmmmmmmh,* stress fluctuations voiced in unison with his arm-straining body swinging toward the object. But one advance occurred. In contrast with requests for near objects, there was now an alternation in gaze between object-locus and mother.

But for all that, the mothers were often unable to figure out what their sons wanted. As a result, they questioned them harder about *what* was wanted (Table 5.2). The child, in a sense, was forced into nominals to get the job done—not because the mother insisted, but for good functional reasons. In fact, the exchange

Table 5.2 • MOTHERS' VERBAL RESPONSES TO JONATHAN'S AND RICHARD'S REQUESTS FOR REMOTE/ABSENT OBJECTS AT VARIOUS AGES

	Child's Age in Months 14–16 17–18 21–24			Examples of Mothers' Typical Utterances in Each Category
Percent type of question or topic of utterance by mother				
Closed yes-no question dis-ambiguating referent	46	36	24	Do you want your book? Is this what you were after?
Open "what" question about referent	18	11	5	What do you want? Where is it?
Open question for more infor-mation about task / goal	3	5	12	Where are you going?
Imposing conditions on request	3	37	25	Darling, it's *not time.* You've got some. You can't have more.
Marking uptake of request	15	5	22	Alright. I'll get it. I'll bring you some more.
"Phonology" and "politeness" lessons by repetition	10	5	9	Not sauceman, sauce-pan, with a *p, p* in the middle. *Thank* you.
Other	5	1	3	(not directly related to request; e.g., You're not by any chance "ya"?)
Total requests by child	8	4	9	
Total utterances by mother	39	19	45	
Mean adult utterances per request	4.8	4.8	5.0	

between them becomes more interpersonal. The child not only looked more often toward his mother when making a remote request; he was now more likely to acknowledge receipt of the object. In roughly six of ten displaced requests, Richard "acknowledged" with an excited, "pleased" *aah-huh*—a prolonged version of his acknowledgment for near objects. Smiling also occurred in about one-third of Richard's displaced requests, and even Jonathan produced the occasional smile in acknowledgment. Both children seemed to be more sensitive to the mother's role as a voluntary agent in complying with requests. I think this may have had to do with their recognition of her uncertainty in figuring out what they were asking for.

Jonathan left us at eighteen months. Richard, by that age, was regularly requesting with nominals. Even at sixteen months, he asked for a book on a far shelf by combining *ghuk* with his ostensive reach. At eighteen months, familiar food and drink from the kitchen were regularly labeled—e.g., *ghikhi* and *an-ni* for biscuit and juice respectively. So too familiar but distant toys like *Teddy*. These nominals were always combined with an initial ostensive reach. But by twenty-one months (when he had a good stock of nominals) he *began* a request for the first time not with a reach but with one of his nominals. *Sos-man* (saucepan) was spoken *before* he gestured requestively for it. And shortly after, request gesturing dropped out altogether. The nominal alone sufficed though no distinctive request intonation had yet been imposed on it. Only when his nominal lexeme failed to communicate did he revert to gestures. And these were accompanied by such vocatives as *mummy; get up; need mummy.* In fact, Richard was moving from object request to requests for supportive action—e.g., steering his mother toward his goal, which we shall discuss later.

A word about "canonical locus," an idea first discussed by John Lyons. It is, I suppose, a classical deictic procedure. Both children began displaced requesting on objects to be found at standardized locations: food, drink, and books. Until seventeen months, for example, nearly all Richard's displaced requests were for books, habitually lodged on a high shelf. Once he began using nominals, these requests exploded in diversity. For they were no longer tied to place. But nonetheless, it was for place-tied book, biscuit, and juice that Richard used these first nominals, though he knew perfectly well where they were and how to indicate their canonical locus. The first nominals used in this way were *not* adopted out of sheer necessity.

Table 5.2 summarizes how the mothers responded to their children's displaced requests. More than half the responses up to eighteen months were about reference: *What do you want? Do you want a book?*, etc. As Richard came to use words more proficiently in the last quarter of his second year, his mother's emphasis shifted. She began to press for refinements in phonology. His request for a *sos-man* was countered with *No, not sauce-man, saucepan, with a 'p', 'p' in the middle!* And she began asking for real words rather than for his "baby" ones.

RICHARD: (points to ball in fireplace, requesting) ogho-wa-wa-wa-wa
MOTHER: Fire
RICHARD: wa
MOTHER: Don't say "wa-wa." Fire, Richard.
RICHARD: Fire
MOTHER: That's better.

But more strikingly, displaced requesting proves fertile ground for enforcing felicity conditions. More than a third of the mothers' responses at a year and a half had to do with "speech act lessons," and a quarter of them thereafter. In the main, these lessons were the standard ones about felicity conditions.

(1) Requests must reflect a genuine need for help. Don't request objects that you can obtain on your own:

You want your car, don't you? Why not make a bit of effort and try and get it?

Nor must he ask for things he already has:

JONATHAN: (still chewing on biscuit, indicates that he wants another)
MOTHER: You haven't finished that one yet, have you? You're still eating it.

JONATHAN: unmmmmmmmh (reaching again)

MOTHER: You're getting to be a greedy little boy, aren't you!

JONATHAN: (turns to mother then points again) mmmmmmh
                  (reaches with other hand) mm-uuh

MOTHER: Mummy'll give you another half when you've fin-
                  ished that one. mm. Have you finished that one?

(2) "Timetable" conditions must be honored. Mother replied
to Richard's request for a biscuit between meals, *Darling, it's not
time.* Upon Richard's persistence, his mother continued:
> *Do you want a drink? . . . If you want a drink you can have one.
> . . . Do you want a drink? Because that's all you're having. . . .*

And when Richard still frets:
> *That's your fault because you didn't eat enough breakfast.*

In this case, not only did she teach timetabling but she also introduced the idea of a substitution, offering an alternative to his
inappropriate request.

(3) Requests must not demand unreasonable effort from others. The child should not, for instance, expect his mother to make
a journey for things that are not really necessary:
> *You want your other book. Well, that's upstairs.*

(4) The voluntarism of the requestee must be respected in
the child's requests. The mother reminds him that her role is
that of a "voluntary agent" by emphasizing the use of ingratiatives and by uttering an exaggerated *thank you* as she grants the
request.

(5) Finally, when the mother cannot or will not comply, she
expects her child to understand and accept her verbal *reasons*
where previously she relied on distracting him by simply supplying an alternative object:

RICHARD: (holds cup out to mother) more

MOTHER: You've got some. You can't have more.

RICHARD: (gestures toward bookshelf)

MOTHER: What are you expecting to come from up there?
                  Hmm? There aren't any more books, you know.

RICHARD: (setting out plates and spoons at pretend tea party)
more . . . (—) spoons (runs toward kitchen)
MOTHER: But we've got enough spoons, one for each plate.
RICHARD: plate (returns to mother, smiling)
MOTHER: Each plate has a spoon.
RICHARD: (resumes tea party)

In other contexts, as we shall see, she requires *him* to give reasons.

In a variety of ways, then—and some quite subtle—these mothers teach their children just as they are on the brink of lexico-grammatical speech that requests *ask* rather then *compel,* that they are made only for services that one cannot do for oneself, and that they must not demand "excessive" effort from another. Requests, she also makes plain early on, relate to timetables and scarcity conditions. They are, moreover, accountable: they can be justified by reasons, of which more presently. The "lessons" are obviously as much cultural as they are linguistic. But language use is principally what culture is about.

So at the end of this first round of examining the simplest form of request—asking for objects—we are forced to a tentative conclusion. Language acquisition appears to be a by-product (and a vehicle) of culture transmission. Children learn to use a language initially (or its prelinguistic precursors) to get what they want, to play games, to stay connected with those on whom they are dependent. In doing so, they find the constraints that prevail in the culture around them embodied in their parents' restrictions and conventions. The engine that drives the enterprise is not language acquisition per se, but the need to get on with the demands of the culture. This point should be so obvious as to need no comment. But in point of fact, unless one keeps one's eye on the pragmatics of language, it can be easily overlooked. Leslie Stephen once made the point that people are not melancholy because they invented Hell. They invented Hell because they were melancholy. Children begin to use language, by the same token, not because they have a language-using capacity, but because they need to get things done by its use. Parents assist them in a like spirit: they want to help them become "civilized" human beings, not just speakers of the language.

Once they begin to use language in this "civilized" way, they then become creatures of the language, swayed by its cultural and linguistic constraints just as surely as men in the Middle Ages were swayed and formed by the concept of Hell.

When developmental linguistics ignores this evident truth, it risks becoming remote from the motives and shaping forces that control the course of language acquisition.

Invitations to Joint Action

Our children seem to use three forms of "invitational" request: (a) an asymmetrical one where the adult is requested to serve as "agent," the child being the "experiencer," as in "book reading"; (b) a parallel one where the child and adult *share* an experience or action, as when the child requests that his mother look out the window with him at the snow or help him to carry something; and (c) an alternating one—i.e., an invitation to a game in which the child and adult take turns, as when the mother builds a structure with blocks and the child then knocks it down. None of these forms of request seemed to be "earliest" or most frequent.

The earliest invitations took the form of "acting out" by the child. In this primitive form the child simulates a part of the action desired, like bouncing up and down on his parent's knee to get the adult to bounce him by his own action. Meredith Crawford has observed such behavior in young chimpanzees attempting to recruit the help of another animal in pulling in a baited box too heavy for one animal to manage alone. The requesting animal simulates pulling on the rope attached to the box when the other is looking his way. Richard not only bounced on his father's knee to request "ride-a-cock-horse," but he pushed the microphone toward him to get him to take a turn talking into it. Such invitations are usually accompanied by vocalizations that are notably less insistent than those accompanying object requests or requests for supportive action. Jonathan often uses his standard *hummh* form, but with a gently rising and falling pitch. Other odd sounds occur: *nyah-no* (medium pitch) and *da-pe* (pitch rising, questioning) at thirteen months for book reading; *neah, nngah, nn* at eighteen months when inviting father to join in play with lego, etc. But little vocal standardization developed. With increasing age, the babbling accompanying invitations became longer and sounded more sentencelike in intonation.

Invitations, perhaps because they were less stereotyped in vocal accompaniment, contained more linguistically advanced forms than the other two types of requests at all ages. The first rudiments of two-word grammar occurred in the invitation format. By twenty-two months, for example, Action-Object or Agent-Action combinations were occurring regularly: *down-slide, mummy-ride, Eileen-do, brrm-brrm-boo-knee* (*brrm-brrm* was what adults said when bouncing Richard on their knees), etc. *More* then became a pivot word for recurrence with nominals, again used first in the invitational format. This format was also the first in which negation was used to indicate unwillingness to continue a joint enterprise: *no ride, no like.* And the first linguistic ingratiatives occurred in invitation formats: *nice mummy, please mummy.*

How to account for this precocity? For one, invitational formats are playful: the heat is off. Outcome is not so crucial. The situation, being more relaxed, also leaves time and more processing capacity for managing communication. Perhaps too, the familiarity of most invitational formats puts less demand on processing capacity, so that richer grammatical combinations can be constructed. And finally, of course, adults were often so charmed at being invited by the child that they responded in a particularly supportive manner. How could they be churlish? Our records show that adults accepted 95 percent of the children's invitations

until the children were sixteen months old. Acceptance declined
after that, when the children were being urged to be more independent. But even so, acceptances were almost always cheerful:
Come on; all right then; let's go.

Perhaps, too, the spirit of an invitation engenders in the
recipient less of a pedagogical reaction, and that itself may min-
imize the child's anticipation of being "put down." Mothers, for
example, exert fewer pressures on the inviting child to fulfill
felicity conditions on request. It is the child's show. Not one
recorded adult response to an invitation in either child's corpus—from mother, father, or observer—challenged the ade-
quacy of the child's requestive procedure!

Increasingly, as the children grew older, adults elaborated
on invitations so as to supply the child with linguistic cues—
though not in a pedagogical spirit:

Are you bringing another book for mummy to look at?
What can we find in this book?
Yes, I'll give you a ride.
Okay, I'm going to draw a . . .

At other times responses would take the form of comments on
the child's implied topic. The child takes the observer to the
radiator to put her hand to it:

OBSERVER: ' Ooh, it's hot!

Even when the adult *must* ask the child to clarify, her questions
are more in the spirit of genuine (rather than pedagogical)
requests for directions or information.

What have I got to do now?
Have I got to put it together?
Are you going to put the others on for Teddy?

And, as such, they provide the child with useful language forms.

Invitations, then, have the property of real "adultlike" reciprocity. They occur in familiar settings free of pressures and in
formats already rich in language usage. They provide a setting
that seems to be extraordinarily rich for the growth of language.

Requests for Supportive Action

Requests for assistance in carrying out the child's goal-directed *actions* are initially fraught with difficulties. The child, as already noted, must combine his knowledge of means-end relations in the real world with the communicative procedures for gaining help in executing them. Knowing how to ask for help implies knowing at least some of the arguments of action involved in the task, if *not* in a linguistic sense, then in a conceptual one. It is not surprising, then, that early supportive requests depend heavily for their success upon adult interpretation. Thwarted in carrying out their own actions, the children began typically by giving the action over to somebody to "repair" it or somehow get it back on course. They left it to the adult to perform the needed task analysis.

There were three kinds of request for supportive aid: for *precision* assistance (to get a box opened, a toy assembled, something unscrewed); for *power* assistance (to free a wedged push-cart, to bring a chair indoors, to open a cupboard door); and for *translocational* assistance (to get from a sitting to a standing position, to get down from a chair, to be lifted to see out the window).

The earliest requests were, of course, translocational—to be lifted up, etc. They were not very frequent or particularly interesting. Supportive requests of the other two types exploded at seventeen to eighteen months, when they constituted 41 percent of all requests made by the two children. Their rise coincided less with a new spurt of sensorimotor competence (none was notable then) than it did with a new appreciation of the role of the adult as a possible instrument in one's own enterprises.

The children literally started by bringing incomplete "tasks" to an adult for "fixing"—e.g., a rundown music box that needed winding up. Jonathan handed it over to his mother, waited for completion, and then reclaimed it. Handing over was peremptory (although often accompanied by babbling) and, if the adult

got right to work on the task, the child was patient—in marked
contrast to the usual impatience displayed while waiting for an
adult to fetch a remote or absent object that the child had
requested. Repossession of the repaired object was made without a glance toward the mother. Here is the twenty-five second
episode in which Jonathan (fifteen months) gets his mother to
rewind his music box:

JONATHAN: (holds music box; looks at box; then at mother)
  MOTHER: (chatting with observer)

JONATHAN: mm
  MOTHER: (continues talking with observer)
JONATHAN: (looks at box; tries to wind it; turns to mother)

hmmm   (tries to wind box; looks at mother; crawls

to mother) eeh, eega, hmmm (holds box out to
mother)
  MOTHER: (reaches toward box)
JONATHAN: (withdraws box; demonstrates attempt to wind;

hands box to mother) here
  MOTHER: Do you want mummy to turn it for you? Look.
(demonstrates how to wind)
JONATHAN: (looks at observer; then watches mother winding.
As soon as music starts, Jonathan reaches and takes
back the box, turning away without acknowledgment)

"Handover" of the task by the child gets elaborated in two
ways; both are instances of "gap indicating." One is a *locative*
procedure: indicating *where* the trouble is by touching a missing
or broken part as in the preceding example. The second is
instrumentive: proposing an instrument needed for effecting a
repair. The latter is more advanced and occurs much later. The
following is from Richard's corpus at twenty-one months.

RICHARD: (examining knob of pan lid) oh-oh, ah scoo

MOTHER: Screw!
RICHARD: (handles lid; screw falls out and knob drops off;
looks up at mother) hah-hah
MOTHER: Yes, now there is a hole!
RICHARD: (holds up lid and knob to mother) hah-heh . . . hole
hole hole
MOTHER: You've broken it.
RICHARD: (holds up lid and knob to mother) broke broke broke
(insistent)
MOTHER: You'll have to get a screwdriver.
RICHARD: ooh screw driver (hands mother lid and knob,
grunting)
MOTHER: Do you want me to get a screwdriver?
RICHARD: (—) broke broke driver (insistent)
MOTHER: Shall I get the screwdriver from the kitchen?
RICHARD: (gives a fretting moan)
MOTHER: And then we can mend it.
RICHARD: (looks at lid in mother's hands) screw screw (insis-
tent wail)
MOTHER: (goes to fetch screwdriver)
RICHARD: (remains sitting on floor, babbling to himself during
mother's absence) acoo dider (screw driver) scoo
diver scoo diver scroo scroo scroo scroo . . . (still
babbling when mother returns with screwdriver)

The request for assistance was, as it were, interpolated in the
task. When his mother finished helping him, Richard went on
playing on his own.

The next development (Richard at twenty-two months)
involved requesting aid while the action was in progress, in order
to *keep* it in progress. The assistance required was virtually a part
of the task being undertaken by the child and required his mother's prolonged intervention. She had, moreover, to be guided.
Such guided requesting occurred only when the child had a plan
of action that he could not communicate or even formulate in

advance. He was led, consequently, to sequence his requests, to lead the adult from one step to the next. Richard began, as shown in the following example, by recruiting help with the vocative *mummy*. When his mother replied *mummy do what?*, he followed with *mummy get up*. His mother then asked, *What do you want mummy to do?* Richard then indicated the locus of the action to be carried out by a gesture and by *Up cupboard* as he took hold of the cupboard door. His mother then insisted upon a "goal" before she would move into the task. His requests, she insisted, must contain "disclosure in advance" about goals. This had the effect of forcing Richard to "assemble" his request in advance of action. Here is the episode in full:

RICHARD: mummy, mummy
MOTHER: (remains seated) What?
RICHARD: muh, mummy   mummy come   (points briefly to the cupboard)
(section omitted)
RICHARD: (steps up to cupboard, one door of which is open and the other, bolted shut. Throughout the following, Richard alternates between looking at mother and looking into cupboard, touching the closed door, or putting his hand just inside the open half) up, up—up
MOTHER: Up the cupboard?
RICHARD: cupboard
MOTHER: What do you mean, "up cupboard"?
RICHARD: up cupboard; up cupboard; up cupboard up
MOTHER: Do you want me to get up?
RICHARD: get up
MOTHER: (mother and observer laugh)
RICHARD: cupboard; cupboard; cupboard-up, cupboard-up, cupboard-up, cupboard-up
MOTHER: (gets up, joins Richard beside cupboard) I can't pick the cupboard up!(opens cupboard, talking softly to Richard)

RICHARD: (stands squirming, looking down. Looks into cupboard, spies a toy telephone) telephone

MOTHER: How about those two telephones? You get out the telephone and make a telephone call. (starts to walk away; cupboard door swings shut again)

RICHARD: mummy (goes to mother, pulls her by the hand toward the cupboard) mummy get out telephone (tries to reopen cupboard, then watches mother)

MOTHER: (props door open) There we are! You get the telephone out then.

RICHARD: (reaches into cupboard) plates out (excited)

MOTHER: mm?

RICHARD: plates out

MOTHER: plates out!

RICHARD: (extracts plates from cupboard, carries them back to sofa, looking up to mother and smiling)

Obviously, we can't know what was initially on Richard's mind. He was plainly having difficulty assembling a full request in advance. He finally got his mother to the cupboard, and did he just happen to see a toy telephone there that distracted him from his initial goal? He was probably in search of a set of plates to use in a tea party for his animals. Yet when the telephone came into view—and he was invited to make a "call"—he produced the full sentence *mummy get out telephone*. But once the door was fully opened, he reverted to his original goal and demanded *plates out*, repeating to his mother *mm?* He did not lack displacement in his speech: he *was* indeed able to ask for out-of-sight objects at this age. The basic difficulty was probably that he could not fully assemble in advance *both* the required plan of action and the communicative request.

By twenty-four months such "successive guidance" had become his habitual mode for requesting complex aid. He typically began by naming the intended agent and an action (*mummy come*). Then a locus was added if needed and occasionally an instrument. This is illustrated by a two-minute episode. Richard was again holding a "tea party" for his toy animals Teddy and Rabbit. He was on the sofa beside his mother and had several times before requested and received cutlery from the kitchen for the "meal," including several spoons, e.g., *red spoon, granny spoon.*

RICHARD:　(leaves sofa, goes across the room toward kitchen door, stands looking into kitchen, then points to it) that spoon (shouting) (turns to mother, still pointing to kitchen) that spoon
MOTHER:　(no response)
RICHARD:　(returns to sofa, grinning; adjusts Teddy's position) Teddy, teddy (steps up to mother at other end of sofa; tries to pull mother by the hand toward kitchen)
MOTHER:　What do you want me to do?
RICHARD:　(points to kitchen, looking from mother to kitchen) that spoon
MOTHER:　Which spoon?
RICHARD:　(still pointing to kitchen, tugging mother's hand, looking to mother) those
MOTHER:　(laughs)
RICHARD:　(tugs hard on mother's hand) mummy, get up (pleading)
MOTHER:　Would you help me? (laughing)
RICHARD:　(moves behind mother, pushes her shoulder) mummy (whining)
MOTHER:　(laughs)
RICHARD:　(comes in front of mother, touches her arm.) mummy get up (insistent) (steps back toward kitchen, arm outstretched to mother)
MOTHER:　What is it you want?
RICHARD:　(approaches mother; touches her arm, smiling) mummy get up (cuddles up to mother's shoulder)

MOTHER: What do you want?

RICHARD: (pulls on mother's shoulder) mummy get up (insistent) (touches mother's collar; smiles; steps back)
mummy get off; need mummy (insistent) (steps to
mother again)

MOTHER: Do you want some more spoons?

RICHARD: more spoons (touches mother's shoulder; Richard
distracted by mother's dress for thirty seconds;
reaches for mother's hand; pulls it; lets go; looks at
mother; pulls her hand again, looking between
kitchen and mother) mummy get off (complaining)
(tugs hard on mother's hand)

MOTHER: (gets up, Richard pulling) right!

RICHARD: (lets go mother's hand; runs ahead to kitchen) right

MOTHER: (follows Richard to kitchen)

RICHARD: (returns with spoons) there; that spoon

Successive guidance slowly merges into full requesting with
goal and means specified in advance. Both Richard's action
"scripts" and his grammar improved sufficiently for him to
assemble complex sentences to match complex requirements.
Richard began "grammaticalized" requesting at the very end of
his second year. Searching unsuccessfully in a pile of games for
a jigsaw puzzle depicting a dog "Dougal," he called across the
room (at twenty-four months): *mummy, look.* Mother made no
move. He ran to her, putting his hand on hers, repeating *mummy.*
She asked, *What do you want me to do:* He ran back to the pile of
games, pointed to them, and said *mummy find Dougal.* Not a fault-
less performance, but there is no question that he now understood and could act on the requirements imposed by the mother's
What do you want me to do? His reply was impeccable.

Supportive requests, then, work their way to a maturity in
which the child can both analyze the task in which he is engaged
and, at the same time, muster the necessary grammar to construct a request in aid of its completion. Requests of this order

(almost always couched in a declarative form) are quintessentially case grammatical in the sense that they require such specifications of the Agent, the Action, and the Object, and, optionally, the Instrument, the Location, and the Recipient. If one restricted the analysis of the corpus of speech to supportive requests only, one would surely conclude that the arguments of action provided a kind of protosemantic generative base for the child's language. But we should have been warned against any such facile conclusion by the preceding chapter, where joint attention figured as a framework far more prominently than did joint action.

Some Conclusions

Requesting, like reference, goes through a negotiatory course toward socialization, whatever its form. Like reference, too, it is contextualized in conventional formats that conform as much to cultural as to linguistic requirements.

In object request the principal task is to incorporate reference into request. When the child finally masters nominals, he need no longer depend upon the interpretive prowess of his mother or the deictic power of his indexical signaling. The demands of dealing with displaced reference in requesting objects provide an incentive. Both children took naturally to nominal referring, *not* because their ostensive, deictic requests failed (for they mostly did not) but out of some built-in preference for more economical procedures. Indeed, displaced requests would probably not have grown so rapidly had it not been for the mastery of referring nominals.

But while each child was mastering the skills of specifying the objects he wanted, he was also mastering the felicity conditions that constrain the making of requests. Needed pragmatic accomplishments were usually firmly in place in advance of each child's referential progress. The "heat" was on the felicity issue, not on the referential one. Invitational requests were exceptions. They were issued only for activities that were already framed in well-shaped, gamelike formats. And reference was no big issue.

Nothing much need be specified when one invites another to play a well-known game. Nor was it a big job to assemble a plan of action while concurrently figuring out how to communicate it.

There is an irony in all this. For while invitations *required* less complexity of utterance than did other forms of request, we already know that they produced the most complex speech samples of all three request types—a matter already discussed. Whether one explains the superiority by reference to minimal stress, increased familiarity, released processing capacity or whatever, it was plain that when one was secure enough to invite, one had the courage as well to try out new forms.

What is most evident about supportive requests is that they require putting together a real-world plan and an appropriate utterance. Many of the children's difficulties were imposed by cultural conventions of requesting to which children also have to conform. The complexity of these conventions was nicely illustrated by the requirement that the objective of a request needs to be disclosed in advance—no easy task for an eighteen-month-old, even in a familiar setting.

Finally, I want to reiterate that learning how to request is not just learning language or even just speech acts. It is also learning the culture and how to get things done by language in that culture. The child knows an enormous amount about the cultural conditions of requesting a year before he knows how to deploy the grammatical inversion rule for framing a question. Indeed, he uses the declarative form exclusively, declaring his requests rather than putting them in query form. Yet his subtlety in meeting both real-world "physical" constraints and culturally elaborate felicity conditions grows apace.

Learning How to Talk

W E BEGAN WITH A SURVEY OF the "original mental capacities" that might help the child in his career as an aspirant speaker of his native tongue. Four were offered as
particularly important: (a) means-end readiness; (b) a sensitivity
to transactional enterprises; (c) systematicity in organizing experience; and (d) abstractness in rule formation. These are not
"capacities" that somehow transform themselves into a formal
system of language by dint of some mysterious process of semi-
otization or even by "simple" socialization. They seem, rather, to
be the minimal mental equipment that a child would need to *use*
language—a matter better treated in a moment.

No doubt the aspirant speaker of a language requires far
more mental machinery than this at the outset to "get into" the
formal, abstract rules that govern his local language. Whatever
other machinery the child must have to get into grammar we
shall simply take for granted. It may include innate knowledge
of a universal grammar, as Chomsky suggested, or it may be in
the form of initial sensitivities to distinctions in both language
and in the real world, as Bickerton has proposed. Such questions
are not the central ones of this book.

Whatever original *language* endowment may consist of and
however much or little of it there may be need not concern us.
For whether human beings are lightly or heavily armored with
innate capacities for lexico-grammatical language, they still have
to learn how to *use* language. *That* cannot be learned *in vitro*. The
only way language use can be learned is by *using* it communicatively. The "rules" of language use are only lightly specified by
the rules of grammar. Well-formedness does not make utterances either effective or appropriate or felicitous. Not that such
rules are not of deep interest: they may tell much about the shape
of mind. It is only that infants learning language are *not* aca-

demic grammarians inferring rules abstractly and independently of use.

Whatever else language is, it is a systematic way of communicating to others, of affecting their and our own behavior, of sharing attention, and of constituting realities to which we then adhere just as we adhere to the "facts" of nature. Let us not be dazzled by the grammarian's questions. Pragmatic ones are just as dazzling and just as mysterious. How indeed do we ever learn to get things done with words?

The central thesis of the preceding chapters—theoretical and empirical alike—has been that there is a Language Acquisition Support System that frames the interaction of human beings in such a way as to aid the aspirant speaker in mastering the uses of language. It is this system that provides the functional priming that makes language acquisition not only possible, but makes it proceed in the order and pace in which it ordinarily occurs. Undoubtedly, there is something in the human genome that predisposes human beings to interact with each other communicatively in just this way—although again, it is not our object to separate the innate from the acquired, the natural from the cultural. Rather, the inquiry has been directed to several crucial linguistic functions and to the interactional settings in which children learn to master them.

As we have seen, the Language Acquisition Support System (let us use the acronym LASS for it) is by no means exclusively linguistic. It is a part, a central feature of the system by which adults pass on the culture of which language is both instrument and creator. For in the privileged interaction of early language, the child has his first opportunity for interpreting "cultural texts." Learning "how to say it," he also learns what is canonical, obligatory, and valued among those to whom he says it. He learns this first and simply in a communicative medium short of language.

A principal vehicle of the Language Acquisition Support System is what we have called a *format*. A format is a standardized, initially microcosmic interaction pattern between an adult and an infant that contains demarcated roles that eventually become reversible. They become, as noted in earlier chapters, such familiar routines in the child's interaction with the social world that they are deserving of James Joyce's term, "epiphanies of the ordinary." They have a scriptlike quality that involves not only action but a place for communication that constitutes, directs, and completes that action. Given that play is the culture of childhood, it is not surprising that formats often have a playful, gamelike nature. In time and with increasing systematicity, formats are assembled into higher-order subroutines and in this sense can be conceived of as the modules from which more complex social interaction and discourse are constructed. In time and with increasing abstractness, formats become like moveable feasts. They are no longer tied to specific settings but can be "imposed" by illocutionary devices on a variety of situations. When they reach this more evolved form, they can properly be called speech acts in the Austinian sense.

In Chapter 3 we considered the gamelike nature of some early formats—literally games like object exchange, peekaboo, hide-and-seek. Such games provide a type case for the framing of early communication. For not only do they fill the bill as role-structured transactional microcosms in which words produce, direct, and complete the action, but they have certain crucial languagelike properties of their own. They are, within their bounds, languagelike "ways of life." What makes them like language is, of course, the presence of a deep structure (e.g., appearance and disappearance), but also the presence of a surface structure, a restricted but highly variable set of means for realizing the deep structure. In this sense, they are abstract and systematic, but they also are tied together by a means-end structure. And in their very nature, given the roles assigned in them, they are transactional. When words are used in such games, they perforce enter into a surface-depth relationship that is already established.

What soon became apparent in our exploration of these game formats was that they eventually migrated from their original situational moorings and were generalized to activities and settings in which they had never before occurred. In time, the child was able to turn virtually any situation into a kind of hide-and-seek. This "detachability" of form from context confirms one in claiming the abstractness of children's early behavior. By the same token, the child's early capacity in games for role sharing and role reversal makes one doubt seriously the claim that *all* early social behavior is egocentric. Indeed, it is highly doubtful that children could learn language as we have observed it were they either irreversibly concrete or implacably egocentric. Nor could they ever play games as they do.

In Chapter 4 we plunged into a classic problem of language—*reference*. In games like peekaboo and hide-and-seek the referent of any expressions used is inherent in the "moves of the game" and need not be specified. Expressions used in games are principally performative. They produce, order, and complete the action just as surely as a dubbing ceremony creates a knight. But in communicative encounters involving reference, however ritualized, one element of the "ceremony" is *not* fixed. The unknown is the referent to which a joint focus of attention is to be achieved by the two participants.

I made the bold claims that the "intent to refer" is unlearned and that so too is the recognition of that intent in others. These claims seem to pose no great problem in the establishment of joint reference. Some basis for referential intersubjectivity must exist before language proper appears. Logically, there would be no conceivable way for two human beings to achieve shared reference were there no initial disposition for it. There is nothing more (or less) mysterious about this unlearned "othermindedness" than there is about the ethologist's contention that members of any species regard other organisms as conspecifics and act accordingly. It is a primitive that "other minds" are treated as if they were like our own minds. Another primitive is that there is a world "out there" that is shared by others. Human beings, I proposed, are born as Naïve Realists, whatever other epistemological conclusions they may achieve later by reasoning. That is the a priori side of it.

But empirical evidence as well as logical necessity supports these claims. How could the infant "know" to follow the line of regard of another to search for a joint visual focus save by knowing it in advance? And how could he spontaneously develop indexical "pointing" without there being some expectancy of its likely effect?

If there is a natural basis for establishing joint attention and a natural way of signaling that one wishes to draw another's attention to what one is experiencing, that still leaves unexplained the *conventionalization* of such activity. For, in fact, *linguistic* reference is *not* natural, and its conventionalization poses a psychological problem. There is a long road between following another's gaze out to an object and being able to comprehend a referring expression like "the cream cheese on the top shelf of the fridge."

I made common cause in Chapter 4 with Hilary Putnam's "historical causal" theory of reference and gave a good list of reasons why a student of the *development* of reference would find his reasoning both useful and compelling. We need not review his arguments about "partial overlap," asymmetry, and the rest. But I would want to add one point to that earlier discussion, one that brings us back to the difference between language use in reference and the more performative use of language in games. In his original presentation Putnam makes much of the "dubbing ceremony" by which some thing or state receives the name "ash tree" or "electricity" or "justice." The burden of the evidence presented in Chapter 4 was that such "dubbing ceremonies" are made and not born. They are created as formats, highly constrained formats that are gradually transformed as the child masters the procedural elements by which the names of objects are indicated. This is first done with nominals placed appropriately in a dialogue format where attention is jointly concentrated on a target.

The dubbing format is made as gamelike by the mother as necessary to accommodate the child's lack of expertise. The degrees of freedom in the format are minimized better to leave capacity available for dealing with the uncertain element of the referent and its indicating nominal. In time, as we saw, the format develops to the point where the two are able even to mark the difference between presupposed referents (i.e., already incorporated in the game) and new ones (not yet in). And once the procedures for referring are firmly enough in place in the format, the mother begins a next step: developing a system of commenting on the referent not simply as an end in itself or to note its existence—*There* it is! or the French *La voila!* or the Italian *Eccole!*—but as a topic to which a comment can be "attached." In fact, the topic-comment structure is probably inherent in the reference format from the start, since the provision of a nominal label by the child or his mother is handled in the dialogue as a primitive nominal predicate on an implicit subject.

If one needed a demonstration of "fine tuning" in language acquisition, the growth of the reference format certainly provides it. The mother restricts the task to the degrees of freedom that she believes the child can handle, and once he shows signs of doing better than that, she raises the level both of her expectancies and of her demands on the child. But to concentrate entirely on the "fine-tunedness" of the mother's implicit pedagogy is really to miss the main point. For the aim of her fine tuning is certainly not refinement for its own sake. It is the achievement of functional appropriateness that she is after. Let me say a word about that.

The mother's objective in the referential format seems to be twofold, and she is prepared to tune her responses to her child with great subtlety to achieve both of them. The first is linguistic in the sense that she is trying to get him first to operate on a primitive semanticity hypothesis that vocalization "stands for" something that the mother and child are sharing visually and to get him to appreciate that there is a *standard* vocalization that is required. These are steps in the direction of becoming a standard speaker of a language. But she also pursues a second cultural goal: communicating to the child that there is a canonical way of negotiating reference, as seen, for example, in little contests over the disambiguation of a referent. Is the figure on an English penny the Queen, the child's grandmother, or simply a lady? The mother exhibits a cultural sensitivity in this negotiation that matches her linguistic fine tuning in accepting or rejecting particular indexical vocalizations. The child is being "trained" not only to *know* the language but to *use* it as a member of a cultural community.

The ontogenesis of procedures of request, treated in Chapter 5, represents yet another step forward. For not only must the child master conventionally acceptable ways of signaling his intention (he came equipped with one such, of course, in being innately endowed with demand crying at the start), but he must incorporate reference into his request. The child does not stay long with the condition in which he signals only *that* he wants, but soon "wishes" to indicate *what* he wants. In effect, he must travel the path from raw demand signaling to the fulfillment of felicity conditions on request. And at the same time, he must combine these achievements with referential ones of increased complexity—displaced referring to absent objects, procedures for referring to punctual and iterative actions, and the like. As his requesting becomes still more complex, he needs to refine it by the addition of a regulatory function (in Michael Halliday's sense) through which he can control *how* his request is to be fulfilled.

Development in all three of the forms of request studied (invitations, requests for objects, and requests for assistance in action) was crucially dependent on conventional framing in familiar formats. It was not that the formats provided any "hints" about the linguistic procedures required by the child, but rather that they provided specifications and "acceptance limits" on what was required. They no more produced the grammatical forms of requesting than the net and the court lines produce the strokes by which a person plays tennis. But just as you have to hit the ball in tennis high enough to clear the net and not so far as to go over the baseline, so in requesting you must specify the end state desired before requesting the means for its achievement, or you must fulfill the essential condition that you cannot yourself do what you requested or the sincerity condition that you really want what you are asking for.

So requesting too provides a means not only of getting things done with words, but of operating in the culture. This entails not only coordinating one's language with the requirements of action in the real world, but of doing so in culturally prescribed ways involving real people. It is not surprising that adults act like full-fledged members not only of the linguistic community (fine-tuned for the occasion), but also as gently demanding members of the culture into which the child must enter. For a very long time, adults are more interested in the child's "manners" than in the linguistic well-formedness of his utterances.

Looking back at the continuity between prelinguistic and later linguistic communication discussed in Chapter 2, a few points would benefit from being gone over again. Recall that four sources of possible continuity were singled out: (a) category correspondence between real world concepts and grammatical forms; (b) continuity between the functions served by prelinguistic and later linguistic communication; (c) the constitutive role of language in forming real world knowledge; and (d) similarity in the cognitive processes by which rules of any sort, linguistic or otherwise, are formed at various ages. What can be said of each of these in the light of the evidence assembled in the preceding chapters?

Concerning sensitization to grammatical forms that correspond to categories of real world knowledge, the preceding discussion has little to say. This is basically an issue in the relation between semantics and syntax and points to the possible "forming" role of the former with respect to the latter. We have only marginally been concerned with such issues.

As to continuity of communicative functions from prelinguistic to early linguistic exchanges, there can be little question of its importance. Continuity of function provides an important scaffold for the development of both referential and requestive procedures. In certain respects, indeed, the continuity of function provides a basis for "progress by substitution." Take the development of reference. The mother for months on end maintains an extraordinarily constant pattern of interacting with the child over the naming of things. The steady format, in effect, holds the function constant. As the child progresses in the mastery of new forms, he substitutes them in the old format to perform the old function. And indeed (as with requests), failure in the use of the new form provokes regression to the older one. Even though the new form may have the effect of transforming and expanding the old function, the continuity remains. Indeed, I rather assume that it is this continuity of function that makes it possible for an adult to "understand" the more primitive forms by which an infant realizes various communicative functions. In this sense, functional continuity provides a basis for adult fine tuning and for the operation of the Language Acquisition Support System.

As for the constitutive role of language, its role in "creating" the world into which the child enters, surely the game formats we examined are constitutive in the deepest sense. Games are literally products of what and how one says things in what contexts. I characterized them earlier as becoming, with development, more systematic and abstract and also as being like "moveable feasts" that can be imposed by speech acts on new situations by invoking the appropriate illocutionary force. Referring, requesting, threatening, promising, etc., are early on the scene as states of the world created in major part by appropriate language use. The source of continuity from constitutiveness was, of course, in the formal structures of language games, which (as I tried to show in Chapter 3) have so many elements in common, from their earliest introduction right on through childhood. It is equally evident, however, that there are major *discontinuities* in development that are created by the constitutive powers of language. We do not treat the child quite as a child any longer when we think him capable of understanding such constitutively based obligations as promising, explaining, being loyal, etc. But even so, the argument still holds that from the very start—and particularly in games—we give the child a running start by introducing him to the constitutive function of language through the use of performatives.

Of conceptual processes common to mind generally and language particularly that give continuity to development, there are few things we can conclude. Our emphasis, rather, has been upon *social* processes that are shared by prelinguistic and linguistic communication. Certainly these processes (turn taking, role interchange, etc.) *do* remain invariant across the change into language and provide a centrally important source of continuity. Indeed, I have even urged that the principal "motive" in language acquisition is the better regulation of these underlying social-cultural processes.

The account of early language acquisition presented in these pages depends heavily on the use of context by both mother and child in forming and interpreting messages. Successful early communication requires a shared and familiar context to aid the partners in making their communicative intentions clear to each other. Indeed, the concept of the format was put forth early in this volume in the hope of explicating how context works in these early communicative encounters.

Oddly enough, the notion of context is rarely explicated in discussions of language. It is a little like the notion of "implicit knowledge"—assumed to be present as a "surround" for explicit knowledge, but not amenable to close analysis. "Text" is what is in words; context is the rest of what affects the interpretation of the words—the "rest" including words and nonwords.

So we will find statements of the following order: (a) To comprehend a sentence is to extract a proposition from it in its context; or (b) A sentence is a device for embedding a proposition in a context. Few attempts have been made to analyze the relations that exist between a sentence, its context, and the proposition that is extracted from their relationship. It is easy enough to specify the sentence *and* the proposition, but what shall be taken as context? Some writers, like Pieter Seuren, urge that we should relax our approach to this issue and observe with admiration the opportunistic ways in which people use context to interpret text. We would be bound to fail if we tried to impose a strict determinism on the process. All these discussions operate under the assumption that the context, like the text, is *there*, there to be interpreted. I want to take a radically different approach to context—what a context "is." Context for the young child cannot be taken as a given, as simply "being there." Operative context, for the child or adult, is selected and constructed. The "rules" or criteria for its selection and construction will, of course, vary with the circumstances. Like rules for forming and transforming the sentences of a text or discourse, the rules for constructing context change with development.

One of the constraints of constructed contexts is that they must be cognitively manageable. That is to say, they must not be so comprehensive as to groan under ordinary conditions of language processing. In speaking or in comprehending speech, we cannot take "everything" into account! If Jane offers John a cup of coffee after dinner and he replies, "Thanks, but I've got to hit the sack early tonight," he is contextualizing his refusal by reference to a (presumably) shared contextualizing presupposition about unmetabolized coffee keeping people awake. The presumption is not a bizarre one, and if Jane bears John no grudge, she will accept his refusal as gracious. The loading is not excessive. But John *could* easily be more contextually demanding by giving a more bizarre response that would force Jane to work intolerably hard in understanding the basis of his refusal—like "No thanks, I'd rather not be a pair of ragged claws." The first implicit rule about constructing context is that it be "ordinary" or "conventional." Reasons for refusing after-dinner coffee should be related to such common matters as caffeine and sleep, not to allusions to the sleepless depression suffered by T. S. Eliot's Prufrock. Ordinariness implies a shared culture.

Another rule of context construction is that we aid the interlocutor in figuring out what we have in mind. There are many "tricks" for accomplishing this. The literature on speech acts can be conceived of as a close analysis of these "tricks" in the sense that John Austin analyzed the subtle means whereby we tell our listeners whether an utterance is to be taken as a commissive, a behabitive, or whatever. But again, mastery of these "tricks" develops with experience in using the language and with negotiating how to interpret meaning. The child's grasp of how to make clear the context of his utterance will certainly be uncertain.

Bearing these two general points in mind, let us redeem the status of formats as specialized versions of contexts. To begin with, formats are preselected and preformed by the mother for the child. They may be varied slightly to keep them "interesting," but they are kept easily recognizable and highly constrained. They are made as gamelike as necessary to restrict them to a set of permissible "moves" that define the context. One sees such nominalizing games as "Where's your nose, eyes, ears, etc.?" or "What's this?" What should be processed from the context has been prearranged by practice and ritualization. Only with mastery of these prearranged contexts does the child or his mother begin to "transfer" the game to a wider set of alternatives. Contextualization starts with manageable and restricted formats and is then extended—and then subjected to further modifications, like bringing them under the sway of the kinds of felicity conditions that govern speech acts.

With respect to the hints by which partners in speech give each other clues about intended context, early formats scarcely need them. They are prefabricated. The labeling format of Chapter 4 is restricted to *books* and *pictures* and *naming*. Early object requests are for things that are already part of habitual interactions—food, toys, pictures. Both eventually are extended to a far broader range and then they come to require disambiguating "hints" about context.

This brings us to conventionalization. The conventions of indicating and requesting, as we have seen repeatedly, are not so much directly linguistic as broadly cultural. When to request, how to prepare the ground, how to address a requestee in order to form a felicitous link—these are what the child learns through interacting. As he masters these "procedures," his signaling of context becomes more "ordinary" and more conventional. And, as a consequence, he can be not context-free in his speech, but context-mobile. That is to say, he can (as already remarked) *impose* a context upon a new situation, indicate how the new situation is to be interpreted by his interlocutor.

How does the process of conventionalization get started? I want to propose that before language proper comes on the scene, the child has "natural" ways of embedding his gestures and vocalizations into contexts of action and interaction. I agree with Arde Denkel's thesis that much of early communicative development consists of converting natural modes of contextualizing into conventional patterns. The natural modes provide the start-up process upon which conventionalization can operate. Let me give some examples.

Take joint attention regulation first. When the young prelinguistic child singles out or touches a "new" object, he often accompanies the act with a protodemonstrative like *da*. Patricia Greenfield reports an interesting sequel to this. One of her subjects used as his next procedure for marking objects of attention the doubled consonant-vowel syllable. Instead of *da*, it would be *bi-bi* or *na-na* or some such. After this stage, the same child marked attended objects with the expression *ada*, with the intonation contour of his mother's expression "What's that?" A "natural" vocal marking shifted first to a "specialized" syllable duplication and then to a more linguistically mimetic form that was well en route to being conventional. From then on, of course, the child went step-by-step into conventional utterance.

Similarly, the study by Scaife and Bruner reported in Chapter 3 indicates that initially the child naturally interprets a "long gaze" in a particular direction as indicating the presence of a visual target to be found along the path of that gaze. But Ryan's study shows that by the end of the first year the child now also interprets conventional rising intonation in the mother's speech as a signal to look for a new visual target. How did the child get from the natural to the conventional in this instance? Unfortunately, we do not have the answer in the form of a research study. But it certainly is not the least inconceivable that it could have jumped the gap by contiguity learning. To argue that the *first* step toward conventionalization is learned does *not* imply that one has embraced once again a thoroughgoing empiricist account of language acquisition. All that it implies is that the child is *ready* and *able* to pick up associated cues that take him into the domain of conventional communicating. To *proceed* in that conventional domain requires the kinds of initial capacities discussed in Chapter 2 as well as some sort of Language Acquisition Device.

Or take an example from demanding and requesting. The child naturally cries when refusing food or an object that is being pressed on him. Other, less natural vocalizations take the place of crying. When conventional negation begins, the first use of "no" is found in the same position as those earlier denial vocalizations. Its contextualization is much the same as its nonstandard predecessors. But now it is amenable to linguistic elaboration (as Roy Pea has shown) by genuine linguistic insights on the part of the child.

Natural contexts are conventionalized into conventional forms and regularized as formats. A format is a routinized and repeated interaction in which an adult and child *do* things to and with each other. Since such formats emerge before lexico-grammatical speech, they are crucial vehicles in the passage from communication to language.

A format is a contingent interaction between at least two acting parties, contingent in the sense that the responses of *each* member can be shown to be dependent on a prior response of the *other*. Each member of the minimal pair has a goal and a set of means for its attainment. Each has the capacity to affect the other's progress toward the respective goals. The goals of the two participants need not be the same; all that is required is that the conditions of communal response contingency be fulfilled.

Formats "grow" and can become as varied and complex as necessary. Their growth is effected in several ways. They may in time incorporate new means or strategies for the attainment of goals, including symbolic or linguistic ones. They may move toward coordination of the goals of the two partners not only in the sense of "agreement," but also with respect to a division of labor and a division of initiative. And they may become conventionalized or canonical in a fashion that permits others within a symbolic community (e.g., a "speech community") to enter the format in a provisional way to learn its special rules.

Formats are also modular in the sense of being accessible as subroutines for incorporation in larger scale, long-term routines. A greeting format, for example, can be incorporated in a larger scale routine involving other forms of joint action. In this sense, any given format may have a hierarchial structure, parts being interpretable in terms of their placement in a larger structure. The creation of higher-order formats by incorporation of subroutine formats is one of the principal sources of presupposition. What is incorporated becomes implicit or presupposed.

Formats, save when highly conventionalized, cannot be specified independently of the perceptions of the participants. In this sense, they generally have the property of contexts in being the resultant of definition by the participants. The definition of formats communally is one of the major ways in which a community or culture controls the interaction of its members. Once a format is conventionalized and "socialized" it comes to be seen as having "exteriority and constraint" in Emile Durkheim's sense and becomes objective in Karl Popper's. Eventually, formats provide the basis for speech acts and their constraining felicity conditions. We learn how to invoke them by speech.

One special property of formats involving an infant and an adult (to pick up Hilary Putnam's point about reference again) is that they are asymmetrical with respect to the knowledge of the partners—one "knows what's up," the other does not know or knows less. Insofar as the adult is willing to "hand over" his knowledge, he can serve in the format as model, scaffold, and monitor until the child achieves requisite mastery.

To sum it up, I see the format as a means for achieving several very crucial pragmatic functions in language acquisition. To begin with, formats embed the child's communicative intentions into a cultural matrix; they are instruments for transmitting the culture as well as its language. Because formats have a sequential structure and a history (as noted earlier), they permit the child to develop primitive concepts of aspectual time. At their simplest, they provide the child with a kind of manageable, middle-range future, defined by the course of the action rather than by abstract time or tense. Because they have an incorporative growth, they become important vehicles for the development of presupposition and for signaling presuppositions. Because they are finite, orderly, and interactive they also provide a context for interpreting what is being said here and now.

One last point. I have tried to set forth a view of language acquisition that makes it continuous with and dependent on the child's acquisition of his culture. Culture is constituted of symbolic procedures, concepts, and distinctions that can only be made in language. It is constituted for the child in the very act of mastering language. Language, in consequence, cannot be understood save in its cultural setting. I hope the account I have set forth has made it clear why the two cannot be treated separately.

NOTES

Preface

p. 7   Austin, J. *How to do things with words*. Oxford: Oxford Univ. Press, 1962.
p. 8   Brown, R. *A first language*. Cambridge, Mass.: Harvard Univ. Press, 1973.
Bloom, L. *One word at a time*. The Hague: Mouton, 1973.
Greenfield, P. & Smith, J. H. *The structure of communication in early language development.* New York: Academic Press, 1976.
Dore, J. A pragmatic description of early language development. *Journal of Psycholinguistic Research*, 1974, *3*, 343–50.
Ryan, J. Early language development. In M. P. M. Richards (ed.), *The integration of a child into a social world.* Cambridge: Cambridge Univ. Press, 1974.
Bruner, J. S. The ontogenesis of speech acts. *Journal of Child Language*, 1975, 2, 1–19.
p. 9   Bruner, J. S. From communication to language. *Cognition*, 1975, *3* (3), 255–87.
Bruner, J. S. A preface to the development of speech. In G. Oleron (ed.), *L'Annee Psychologique: Homage à Paul Fraisse*. Presses Universites de France, 1977.
Ratner, N. & Bruner, J. S. Games, social exchange and the acquisition of language. *Journal of Child Language*, 1978, 5, 391–401.
p. 10 Ninio, A. & Bruner, J. S. The achievement and antecedents of labelling. *Journal of Child Language*, 1978, 5, 1–15.
Bruner, J. S., Caudill, E., & Ninio, A. Language and experience. In R. S. Peters (ed.), *John Dewey reconsidered*. London: Routledge & Kegan Paul, 1977.
Bruner, J. S., Ratner, N., & Roy, C. The beginning of request. In K. Nelson (ed.), *Children's language*, vol. IV. New York: Gardner Press, 1982.
Bruner, J. S. Formats of language acquisition. *American Journal of Semiotics*, 1982, *1* (3), 1–16.
p. 11 Geertz, C. *The interpretation of cultures: Selected essays*. New York: Basic Books, 1973.
Sperber, D. *Rethinking symbolism*. Cambridge: Cambridge Univ. Press, 1973.

O N E / Introduction

p. 17 The epigraph is in Massimo Piattelli-Palmarini, ed., *Language and learning: The debate between Jean Piaget and Noam Chomsky*. Cambridge, Mass.: Harvard Univ. Press, 1980, p. 262. Based on transcripts of a debate held in October 1975, at Abbaye de Royalmont. For general background on the different approaches to the study of language acquisition, the following books will be of particular help:
Austin, J. *How to do things with words*. Oxford: Oxford Univ. Press, 1962.
Bates, E. *Language in context: The acquisition of pragmatics*. New York: Academic Press, 1976.
Beilen, H. *Studies in the cognitive basis of language development*. New York: Academic Press, 1975.
Bever, T. G. The cognitive basis for linguistic structures. In J. R. Hays (ed.), *Cognition and the development of language*. New York: Wiley, 1970.
Bickerton, D. *Roots of language*. Ann Arbor, Mich.: Karoma Publishers, 1981.
Chomsky, N. *Aspects of the theory of syntax*. Cambridge, Mass.: MIT Press, 1975.
Clark, H. H. & Clark, E. V. *Psychology and language: An introduction to psycholinguistics*. New York: Harcourt Brace Jovanovich, 1977.
Cromer, R. The development of language and cognition: The cognition hypothesis.

In B. Foss (ed.), *New perspectives in child development.* Harmondsworth, Eng.: Penguin, 1974.
Cromer, R. Reconceptualizing language acquisition and cognitive development. In R. L. Schiefelbusch & D. Bricker, *Early language: Acquisition and intervention.* Baltimore, Md.: University Park Press, 1981.
De Laguna, G. *Speech: Its function and development.* New Haven: Yale Univ. Press, 1927.
De Villiers, J. & De Villiers, P. *Language acquisition.* Cambridge, Mass.: Harvard Univ. Press, 1978.
Greenfield, P. Structural parallels between language and action in development. In A. Lock (ed.), *Action, gesture and symbol.* London: Academic Press, 1978.
Karmiloff-Smith, A. *A functional approach to child language: A study of determiners and reference.* Cambridge: Cambridge Univ. Press, 1979.
McNeill, D. *The acquisition of language.* New York: Harper & Row, 1970.
McNeill, D. *The conceptual basis of language.* Hillsdale, N.J.: Erlbaum Publishers, 1979.
Pinker, S. Formal models of language learning. *Cognition,* 1979, *7,* 217–83.
Searle, J. *Speech acts: An essay in the philosophy of language.* Cambridge: Cambridge Univ. Press, 1969.
Sinclair-de-Zwart, H. Language acquisition and cognitive development. In T. E. Moore (ed.), *Cognitive development and the acquisition of language.* New York: Academic Press, 1973.
Slobin, D. Cognitive prerequisites for the development of grammar. In C. A. Ferguson & D. Slobin (eds.), *Studies of Child Language Development.* New York: Holt, Rinehart & Winston, 1973.
Trevarthen, C. The foundations of intersubjectivity: Development of interpersonal cooperative understanding in infants. In D. Olson (ed.), *The social foundations of language and thought.* New York: Norton, 1980.

T W O / From Communicating to Talking

p. 23 Chomsky, N. *Reflections on language.* New York: Random House, 1975.
Chomsky, N. Review of *Verbal Behavior* by B. F. Skinner. *Language,* 1959, *35,* 26–58.
Bickerton, D. *Roots of language.* Ann Arbor, Mich.: Karoma Publishers, 1981.
p. 24 For a fuller discussion of these points, see:
Bruner, J. S. Nature and uses of immaturity. In K. J. Connolly & J. S. Bruner (eds.), *The growth of competence.* London & New York: Academic Press, 1974.
p. 25 Kalnins, I. & Bruner, J. S. The coordination of visual observation and instrumental behavior in early infancy. *Perception,* 1973, *2,* 307–14.
Papousek, H. Elaborations of conditioned head-turning. Paper presented at the symposium on Learning of Human Infants, London, 1969.
p. 26 Stern, D. *The first relationship: Infant and mother.* Cambridge, Mass.: Harvard Univ. Press, 1977.
Brazelton, T. B., Kozlowski, B., & Main, M. The origins of reciprocity: The early mother-infant interaction. In M. Lewis & L. Rosenblum (eds.), *The effect of the infant on its caregiver.* New York: Wiley, 1974.
Bruner, J. S. Nature and uses of immaturity. In K. J. Connolly & J. S. Bruner (eds.), *The growth of competence.* London & New York: Academic Press, 1974.
p. 27 Bower, T. G. R. *Perceptual world of the child.* Cambridge, Mass.: Harvard Univ. Press, 1973.
Meltzoff, A. & Moore, M. K. Imitation of facial and manual gestures by human neonates. *Science,* 1977, *198,* 75–78.
Tronick, E. (ed.). *Social interchange in infancy: Affect, cognition and communication.* Baltimore, Md.: University Park Press, 1982.
p. 28 For a discussion of the structure of early action, see:
Bruner, J. S. & Bruner, B. M. On voluntary action and its hierarchical structure. *International Journal of Psychology,* 1968, *3* (4), 239–55.
Bruner, J. S. The organization of early skilled action. *Child Development,* 1973, *44,* 1–11.
Piaget, J. *Structuralism.* London: Routledge & Kegan Paul, 1971.
Piaget, J. *The construction of reality in the child.* London: Routledge & Kegan Paul, 1937.
Werner, H. *Comparative psychology of mental development.* New York: Science Editions, 1961. New York: International Universities Press, 1948.
p. 29 For a discussion of the combinational structure of early play, see:

Koslowski, B. & Bruner, J. S. Learning to use a lever. *Child Development*, 1972, *43* (3), 790–99.
Bruner, J. S. The organization of early skilled action. *Child Development*, 1973, *44*, 1–11.
Weir, R. *Language in the crib*. The Hague: Mouton, 1962.
Bowerman, M. The acquisition of word meaning: An investigation into some current conflicts. In N. Waterson & C. Snow (eds.), *The development of communication*. New York: Wiley, 1978.
The debate on "rich interpretation" of early speech is reviewed in:
Greenfield, P. & Smith, J. H. *The structure of communication in early language development*. New York: Academic Press, 1976.

p. 30 An example of the "surprise reaction" produced by objects that are changed upon reappearance is found in:
Gardner, J. The development of object identity in the first six months of human infancy. Ph.D. Thesis, Department of Social Relations, Harvard University, 1971.
The surprise produced by "unnatural" causation is reported in:
Leslie, A. The representation of perceived causal connection in infancy. D. Phil. Thesis, Department of Experimental Psychology, University of Oxford, 1979.
The transmodal or "amodal" basis for the recognition of objects is reported by:
Bryant, P., Jones, P., Claxton, V., & Perkins, G. Recognition of shapes across modalities by infants. *Nature*, 1972, *240* (5379), 303–304.
Meltzoff, A. Imitation, inter-modal coordination and representation in early infancy. In G. Butterworth (ed.), *Infancy and epistemology*. London: Harvester Press, 1981.
Piaget, J. *Structuralism*. London: Routledge & Kegan Paul, 1971.
These distinctions (e.g., between specific and nonspecific, etc.) are discussed by:
Bickerton, D. *Roots of Language*. Ann Arbor, Mich.: Karoma Publishers, 1981.

p. 31 The Language Acquisition Device is discussed in:
Chomsky, N. Review of *Verbal Behavior* by B. F. Skinner. *Language*, 1959, *35*, 26–58.
Chomsky, N. *Aspects of a theory of syntax*. Cambridge, Mass.: MIT Press, 1965.
Chomsky, N. Explanatory models in linguistics. In E. Nagel, P. Suppes, & A. Tarski (eds.), *Logic, methodology and philosophy of science*. Stanford, Calif.: Stanford Univ. Press, 1962.
Criticism of this idea is contained in an interesting article by:
Levelt, W. J. M. What became of LAD? In *Ut videam: Contributions to an understanding of linguistics*. Festschrift fur Pieter Verburg on the occasion of his 70th birthday. Lisse, The Netherlands: Peter de Ridder Press, 1975.
St. Augustine. *Confessions*. Baltimore, Md.: Penguin Books, 1961.

p. 32 The transformation of Augustinian learning into the modern dress of imitation and reinforcement is more fully discussed in:
Bruner, J. S. The role of dialogue in language acquisition. In A. Sinclair, R. J. Jarvella, & W. J. M. Levelt (eds.), *The child's conception of language*. Berlin: Springer-Verlag, 1978.
The P(O) construction was first introduced by:
Braine, M. D. S. The ontogeny of English phrase structure: The first phase. *Language*, 1963, *39*, 1–13.
Its syntactical status has been cast into doubt by:
Bloom, L. *Language development: Form and function in emerging grammars*. Cambridge, Mass.: MIT Press, 1970.
Bowerman, M. *Learning to talk: A cross-linguistic study of early syntactic development with special reference to Finnish*. Cambridge: Cambridge Univ. Press, 1973.
Brown, R. *A first language*. Cambridge, Mass.: Harvard Univ. Press, 1973.
See:
Skinner, B. F. *Verbal Behavior*. New York: Appleton-Century-Crofts, 1957.
Chomsky, N. Review of *Verbal Behavior* by B. F. Skinner. *Language*, 1959, *35*, 26–58.
Chomsky, N. *Syntactic structures*. The Hague: Mouton, 1957.

p. 34 Miller's remark is discussed in:
Bruner, J. S. Acquiring the uses of language. *Canadian Journal of Psychology/Review of Canadian Psychology*, 1978, *32*, 204–18.
See:
Fillmore, C. The case for case. In E. Bach & R. T. Harms (eds.), *Universals in linguistic theory*. New York: Holt, Rinehart & Winston, 1968.
Fillmore, C. The case for case reopened. In P. Cole & J. M. Seadock (eds.), *Syntax and semantics, Vol. 3: Speech acts*. New York: Academic Press, 1968.

p. 35
Brown, R. *A first language.* Cambridge, Mass.: Harvard Univ. Press, 1973.
See:
Greenfield, P. & Smith, J. H. *The structure of communication in early language development.* New York: Academic Press, 1976.
Nelson, K. Concept, word and sentence: Interrelations in acquisition and development. *Psychological Review,* 1974, *81* (4), 267–85.
Nelson, K. & Gruendel, J. Generalized event representations: Basic building blocks of cognitive development. In A. Brown & M. Lamb (eds.), *Advances in developmental psychology,* vol. 1.

p. 36
For early discussions of the role of "world knowledge" in language acquisition, see:
Olson, D. R. Language and thought: Aspects of a cognitive theory of semantics. *Psychological Review,* 1970, *77* (4), 257–73; and:
MacNamara, J. The cognitive basis of language acquisition in infants. *Psychological Review,* 1972, *79,* 1–13.
de Saussure, F. *Course in general linguistics.* New York: Philosophical Library, 1955.
Wittgenstein, L. *Philosophical investigations.* Oxford: Blackwell, 1953.
Austin, J. *How to do things with words.* Oxford: Oxford Univ. Press, 1962.

p. 37
Brown, R. Introduction. In Snow & Ferguson (eds.), *Talking to children: Language input and acquisition.* Cambridge: Cambridge Univ. Press, 1977.
Searle, J. *Speech acts: An essay in the philosophy of language.* Cambridge: Cambridge Univ. Press. 1969.

p. 38
Snow, C. & Ferguson, C. *Talking to children: Language input and acquisition.* Cambridge: Cambridge Univ. Press, 1977.

p. 40
Bickerton, D. *Roots of language.* Ann Arbon, Mich.: Karoma Publishers, 1981.

p. 41
Grice, H. P. Logic and conversation. In P. Cole & J. Morgan (eds.), *Syntax and semantics,* vol. 3. London: Academic Press, 1975.
Nelson, K. & Gruendel, J. Generalized event representations: Basic building blocks of cognitive development. In A. Brown & M. Lamb (eds.), *Advances in developmental psychology,* vol. 1.
For a discussion of the child's "entry" into the Gricean cycle, see:
Denkel, A. Communication and meaning. D. Phil. Thesis, Department of Philosophy, University of Oxford, 1977.

T H R E E / *Play, Games, and Language*

p. 45
The study of the nature and uses of immaturity is discussed in:
Bruner, J. S. Nature and uses of immaturity. In K. J. Connolly & J. S. Bruner (eds.), *The growth of competence.* London & New York: Academic Press, 1974.
A fuller discussion of such games of childhood and their linguistic implications can be found in:
Bruner, J. S. & Sherwood, V. Early rule structure: The case of "peekaboo." In R. Harre (ed.), *Life sentences: Aspects of the social role of language.* New York & London: Wiley, 1976; and:
Ratner, N. & Bruner, J. S. Games, social exchange and the acquisition of language. *Journal of Child Language,* 1978, *5,* 391–401.

p. 47
Buhler, K. *Sprachtheories: Die Darstellungsfunktion der Sprache.* Jena: Fischer, 1934.

p. 60
Stern, D., Hofer, L., Haft, W., & Dore, J. Interpersonal communication: The attunement of affect states by means of intermodal fluency. Paper presented at the International Conference on Infancy Studies, Austin, Texas, March, 1982; and at the New York Child Language Group Conference, New York, May, 1982.
Kaye, K. & Charney, R. How mothers maintain "dialogue" with two-year-olds. In D. Olson (ed.), *The social foundations of language and thought.* New York: Norton, 1980.
Brazelton, T. B., Kozlowski, B., & Main, M. The origins of reciprocity: Early mother-infant interaction. In M. Lewis & L. Rosenblum (eds.), *The effect of the infant on its caregiver.* New York: Wiley, 1974.

F O U R / *The Growth of Reference*

p. 67
Putnam, H. *Mind, language and reality.* Cambridge: Cambridge Univ. Press, 1975.

p. 68
Ogden, C. K. & Richards, I. A. *The meaning of meaning.* New York: Harcourt & Brace, 1923.

See:

Deutsch, W. & Pechmann, T. Interaction and the development of definite descriptions. Unpublished manuscript, MPIP, Nijmegen, The Netherlands, 1981.

Deutsch, W. & Pechmann, T. Form and function in the development of reference. Paper presented to Symposium 18 (Language Development and Preverbal Communication). XXII International Congress of Psychology, Leipzig, 1980.

Pechmann, T. & Deutsch, W. From gesture to word and gesture. Papers and Reports on Child Language Development. Linguistics Department, Stanford University, 1980.

Pechmann, T. & Deutsch, W. The development of verbal and nonverbal devices for reference. *Journal of Experimental Child Psychology*, 1982, *34*, 330–41.

p. 69 Chance, M. Attention structure as the basis of primate rank orders. *Man*, 1967, *2*, 503–18.

It is to C. S. Peirce that we owe the distinction of indexes, icons, and symbols; see:

Peirce, C. S. *Collected papers*, Cambridge, Mass.: Harvard Univ. Press, (vols. 2 and 5), 1932–34.

p. 70 Lyons, J. Deixis as the source of reference. In E. L. Keenan (ed.), *Formal semantics of natural language*. Cambridge: Cambridge Univ. Press, 1975.

Robson, K. S. The role of eye-to-eye contact in maternal-infant attachment. *Journal of Child Psychology & Psychiatry*, 1967, *8*, 13–25.

Stern, D., Hofer, L., Haft, W., & Dore, J. Interpersonal communication: The attunement of affect states by means of intermodal fluency. Paper presented at the International Conference on Infancy Studies, Austin, Texas, March, 1982; and New York Child Language Group Conference, New York, May, 1982.

p. 72 Lyons, J. Deixis as the source of reference. In E. L. Keenan, (ed.), *Formal semantics of natural language*. Cambridge: Cambridge Univ. Press, 1975.

p. 73 Ryan, M. L. *Contour in context*. Paper presented at the Psychology Language Conference, Stirling, Scotland, 1976.

Scaife, M. & Bruner, J. S. The capacity for joint visual attention in the infant. *Nature*, 1975, *253* (5489), 265–66.

Butterworth, G. What minds have in common in space: A perceptual mechanism for joint reference in infancy. Paper presented to The Annual Conference of the Developmental Psychology Section, British Psychological Society, Southhampton, September, 1979.

Butterworth, G. & Jarrett, N. The geometry of preverbal communication. Paper presented to The Annual Conference, Developmental Psychology Section, British Psychological Society, "Language, Communication and Understanding," Edinburgh, September, 1980.

p 74 Putnam, H. *Mind, language and reality*. Cambridge. Cambridge Univ. Press, 1975.

Hogan, W. Theoretical egocentrism and the problem of compliance. *American Psychologist*, May, 1975, 533–40.

p. 76 I am indebted to Magda Kalmar of the University of Budapest for providing this striking instance of pointing to a "hypothetical" location in space.

p. 77 Ninio, A. & Bruner, J. S. The achievement and antecedents of labelling. *Journal of Child Language*, 1978, *5*, 1–15.

p. 78 Gellman, R. & Shatz, M. Appropriate speech adjustments: The operation of conversational constraints on talk to two-year-olds. In M. Lewis & L. Rosenblum (eds.), *Interaction, conversation and the development of language*. New York: Wiley, 1977.

p. 81 Quine, W. V. *The roots of reference*. La Salle, Ill.: Open Court, 1973.

Schlesinger, I. M. *The acquisition of words and concepts*. Unpublished manuscript, Jerusalem, The Hebrew University, 1978.

p. 82 Grice, H. P. Logic and conversation. In P. Cole & J. Morgan (eds.), *Syntax and semantics*, vol. 3. London: Academic Press, 1975.

p. 84 Chafe, W. *Meaning and the structure of language*. Chicago: Chicago Univ. Press, 1970.

p. 85 For particularly penetrating discussions of how the child might go about mastering the intent of an utterance, see:

Harrison, B. *Meaning and structure: An essay in the philosophy of language*. New York: Harper & Row, 1972.

McShane, J. *Learning to talk*. Cambridge: Cambridge Univ. Press, 1980.

Denkel, A. Communication and meaning. D. Phil. Thesis, Department of Philosophy, University of Oxford, 1977.

Shatz, M. The relationship between cognitive processes and the development of cognitive skills. In B. Keasy (ed.), Nebraska Symposium on Motivation, 1977. Lincoln, Neb.: Univ. of Nebraska Press, 1978.

p. 86   Putnam, H. *Mind, language and reality.* Cambridge: Cambridge Univ. Press, 1975.
p. 87   See Miller's discussion in:
Miller, G. *Spontaneous apprentices.* New York: Seabury Press, 1977.
Carey, S. The child as word learner. In M. Halle, J. Bresnan & G. A. Miller (eds.), *Linguistic theory and psychological reality.* Cambridge, Mass.: MIT Press, 1978.
Bartlett, E. J. The acquisition of the meaning of color terms: A study of lexical development. In R. Campbell & P. Smith (eds.), *Recent advances in the psychology of language: Language development and mother-child interaction.* New York: Plenum, 1978.

FIVE / The Development of Request

p. 91   Hintikka, J. Questions about questions. In M. K. Munitz & P. K. Unger (eds.), *Semantics and philosophy.* New York: New York Univ. Press, 1974.
Katz, J. The logic of questions. In M. K. Munitz & P. K. Unger (eds.), *Semantics and Philosophy.* New York: New York Univ. Press, 1974.
Searle, J. *Speech acts: An essay in the philosophy of language.* Cambridge: Cambridge Univ. Press, 1969.
Garvey, C. Requests and responses in children's speech. *Journal of Child Language,* 1975, *2,* 41–63.
Ricks, D. M. The beginnings of vocal communication in infants and autistic children. Unpublished Doctorate of Medicine Thesis, University of London, 1972.
p. 92   Pratt, C. *The socialization of crying.* Unpublished doctoral dissertation, University of Oxford, 1978.
p. 95   Sugarman, S. Some organization aspects of preverbal communication. In I. Markova (ed.), *The social context of language.* New York: Wiley, 1978.
p. 100 Lyons, J. *Semantics.* Cambridge: Cambridge Univ. Press, 1977. (See especially chapter 15.)
Stephen, L. *History of English thought in the eighteenth century.* London: John Murray, 1902; reprinted 1927.
p. 104 Crawford, M. Cooperative behavior in young chimpanzees. *Psychological Bulletin,* 1935, *32,* 714.
p. 115 The following work came to the author's attention after the current volume was complete:
Haselkorn, S. The development of the requests of young children from nonverbal strategies to the power of language. D. Education Thesis, Graduate School of Education, Harvard University, 1981.

SIX / Learning How to Talk

p. 123 Putnam, H. *Mind, language and reality.* Cambridge: Cambridge Univ. Press, 1975.
p. 125 Halliday, M. *Learning how to mean.* London: Edward Arnold, 1975.
p. 128 Seuren, P. Personal communication.
p. 129 I am indebted to Dan Sperber, whose talk at Princeton University in the spring of 1982 helped form the discussion of context and its construction.
p. 131 Denkel, A. Communication and meaning, D. Phil. Thesis, Dept. of Philosophy, University of Oxford, 1977.
Greenfield, P. & Smith, J. H. *The structure of communication in early language development.* New York: Academic Press, 1976.
Scaife, M. & Bruner, J. S. The capacity for joint visual attention in the infant. *Nature,* 1975, *253* (5489), 265–66.
Ryan, M. L. *Contour in context.* Paper presented at the Psychology Language Conference, Stirling, Scotland, 1976.
p. 132 Pea, R. The development of negation in early child language. D. Phil. Thesis, Department of Psychology, Oxford University, 1978.
p. 133 Durkheim, E. *The elementary forms of the religious life.* New York: Free Press, 1965.
Popper, K. *Objective knowledge: An evolutionary approach.* Oxford: Clarendon Press, 1972.
The discussion of "formats" presented here was first elaborated in:
Bruner, J. S. Formats of language acquisition. *American Journal of Semiotics,* 1982, *1* (3), 1–16.

INDEX